W9-CUX-726

At Issue

The American Housing Crisis

Other Books in the At Issue Series:

Adaptation and Climate Change

Affirmative Action

Animal Experimentation

Are Teen Curfews Effective?

Can Busy Teens Suceed Academically?

Child Pornography

Club Drugs

Do Abstinence Programs Work?

Do Infectious Diseases Pose a Threat?

Do Tax Breaks Benefit the Economy?

Ethanol

The Ethics of Cloning

Fast Food

Is Racism a Serious Problem?

Is Selling Body Parts Ethical?

Nuclear Weapons

Teen Suicide

At Issue

The American Housing Crisis

Susan Hunnicutt, Book Editor

GREENHAVEN PRESS
A part of Gale, Cengage Learning

GALE
CENGAGE Learning

Detroit • New York • San Francisco • New Haven, Conn • Waterville, Maine • London

GALE
CENGAGE Learning

Christine Nasso, *Publisher*
Elizabeth Des Chenes, *Managing Editor*

For more information, contact:
Greenhaven Press
27500 Drake Rd.
Farmington Hills, MI 48331-3535
Or you can visit our Internet site at gale.cengage.com

LIBRARY OF CONGRESS CATALOGING-IN-PUBLICATION DATA

The American housing crisis / Susan Hunnicutt, book editor.
    p. cm. -- (At issue)
  Includes bibliographical references and index.
  ISBN 978-0-7377-4310-4 (hbk.)
  ISBN 978-0-7377-4309-8 (pbk.)
  1. Subprime mortgage loans--United States--Juvenile literature. 2. Housing--United States--Finance--Juvenile literature. 3. Financial crisis--United States--Juvenile literature. I. Hunnicutt, Susan.
  HG2040.5.U5A695 2009
  332.7'220973--dc22
                                              2008039332

Printed in the United States of America
1 2 3 4 5 6 7 13 12 11 10 09

Contents

Introduction 7

1. Understanding the Subprime Crisis 10
   Path to Investing

2. The Subprime Mortgage Crisis Is Destroying 21
   Homes and Neighborhoods
   Jeff Swicord

3. Disregard for Applicants' Incomes Contributed 28
   to the Subprime Problem
   Gretchen Morgenson

4. Wall Street Created the Subprime Problem 33
   Paul Muolo

5. Washington Is Responsible for the 38
   Subprime Crisis
   John Atlas and Peter Dreier

6. The Federal Reserve Board Is Responsible 44
   for the Subprime Crisis
   Tito Boeri and Luigi Guiso

7. The Federal Reserve Board Is Not Responsible 49
   for the Subprime Crisis
   Irwin M. Stelzer

8. Racial Discrimination May Be an Issue in 54
   the Subprime Crisis
   Algernon Austin

9. Many Working Americans Cannot Afford 58
   a Home
   Michael Grunwald

10. The Government Should Focus on Families   **66**
That Have Lost Their Homes
Paul Weinstein Jr.

11. The Government Should Print More   **76**
Money to Free Up Funds for Lending
John H. Makin

12. The Lending Industry Should Be   **81**
Regulated to Protect Consumers
Neal Peirce

13. Smarter Buyers and Tougher Lending   **85**
Standards Are Needed
Hans L. Schwendimann

14. The Government Should Not Bail Out   **92**
Problem Mortgages
David C. John

15. Lenders Should Not Be Allowed to Charge   **97**
More for Mortgages in Poor Areas
Mary Kane

Organizations to Contact   **105**

Bibliography   **109**

Index   **116**

Introduction

In late spring of 2008, the city council of Birmingham, Alabama, announced that it would file suit against multiple unnamed mortgage companies for unfair and deceptive lending practices. The suits were the city's response to an epidemic of foreclosures, large numbers of abandoned homes, and declining property values in neighborhoods across the city. According to Dagney Johnson Walker, the attorney hired to handle the litigation, the subprime mortgage crisis has harmed Birmingham by contributing to blight, or deterioration of the city. In addition to protecting citizens who are not able to speak for themselves, Johnson told the *Birmingham News* the suits were being filed because lower property values and the necessity of maintaining large numbers of abandoned properties constituted an unfair burden on the city.

"We would like to lend our voices to those that have been raised in other cities demanding that these banks cease their predatory lending practices," said Julie Elmer, special counsel for the mayor's office. Those practices include routinely issuing loans based on unverified financial information to customers who did not have the financial resources to repay them. It also is claimed that large numbers of adjustable rate mortgages were issued with terms that were poorly understood by individuals who took them out. Once the rates began to adjust, the houses became unaffordable as families did not have the financial resources to make the rapidly escalating payments.

As foreclosures increased, property values began to decline. In some cases even homeowners who had not fallen behind on their mortgages were nevertheless abandoning their homes because they found themselves tied to loans on property that was now worth less than they had paid for it, in neighborhoods that were falling apart around them.

It is a scenario that has been repeated in communities across the country. At the time of Birmingham's announcement, the cities of Baltimore and Cleveland also were considering lawsuits against lenders. By early summer 2008 three states, California, Illinois, and Florida, had filed lawsuits against Countrywide Financial Corporation, one of the lenders accused of unfair practices. In addition to monetary damages, the Illinois suit asks the court to require that Countrywide rescind or reform all questionable loans issued from 2004 through the present. The suit claims that Countrywide, among other things, made marketing claims, such as its "no closing costs loans" that were false and misleading.

Massachusetts was involved in similar legal actions. In February 2008, a Massachusetts court took the unusual step of requiring one lender to cease all foreclosure activity in order to give state officials time to look at each case individually. In states and cities across the country, government officials were voicing alarm, and looking for ways to protect communities that were being destroyed by unprecedented numbers of foreclosures.

The decision by states and municipalities to focus on the responsibilities of lenders is an attempt to change the direction of the public conversation about the subprime crisis. "Instead of putting the burden on every individual homeowner who got bad loans to prove that it was a predatory loan, the burden shifts to the predatory lender itself to prove that the loan wasn't predatory," said Austin King of the Acorn Financial Justice Center.

In fact, assigning blame for the subprime mortgage crisis has become a complicated and contentious exercise. While states and municipalities have focused on lenders, a large number of other interests have been identified as contributing to a financial crisis that has become international in scope. For example, an article published in *Business Week* magazine in the summer of 2007 identified three different financial interest groups as sharing some measure of responsibility for actions leading to the subprime crisis:

First, according to *Business Week*, Wall Street firms purchased large numbers of subprime loans and bundled them together to create products called collateralized debt obligations (CDOs), which they then sold to investors. The fact that Wall Street was interested in buying subprime debt actually may have helped to create the market for it in the first place.

Then, bond rating agencies like Moody's Investors Service, Fitch Ratings, and Standard & Poor's played up the value and de-emphasized the risks of the CDOs, without really examining their financial viability. Possibly, again according to *Business Week*, the failure of the bond rating agencies to properly evaluate CDOs can be traced to a conflict of interest resulting from the way the bond rating agencies make their money. The role of bond rating agencies was critical because without their statements approving the CDOs, large investors in positions of public trust, such as pension funds and university endowments, would not have been able to invest in them.

Finally, hedge funds, which invested billions of dollars in subprime debt, helped to support a system that at its core was lacking in financial integrity.

As foreclosures have multiplied, the value of the CDOs has plummeted, wiping out billions of dollars of capital, bringing down some large financial institutions like the investment house Bear Sterns, calling into question the financial solvency of others, and leaving investors feeling ripped off.

Finally, the *Business Week* article did point out the poor judgment of homeowners who took out risky loans for property they could not really afford.

How will society finally apportion responsibility for a national financial crisis of such immense proportions, in which one person's guilty party is another person's victim, and in which blame often seems to run in circles? This is one of the key issues addressed in *At Issue: The American Housing Crisis*.

1

Understanding the Subprime Crisis

Path to Investing

Path to Investing is an educational Web site for investors. It is produced by the Securities Industry and Financial Markets Association (SIFMA) Foundation for Investor Education, a not-for-profit organization dedicated to advancing financial knowledge.

Subprime loans were designed for borrowers with weak credit histories. They usually have a low introductory interest rate that later becomes a variable rate. Starting in the early part of this decade, the number of subprime loans issued increased, and housing prices were driven up by the availability of easy credit. As interest rates on these loans have begun to reset, the default rate has risen, and many people have lost their homes. Because the price of housing became inflated as a result of easy credit, the market value of homes is also decreasing. The resulting losses have affected individual homeowners, the broader economy, and the stock market.

The subprime mortgage crisis has dominated the headlines since the summer of 2007. What began as a limited problem affecting high-risk—or subprime—mortgage borrowers in the U.S. has rippled throughout the world financial markets.

Subprime loans are generally made to borrowers who have weak credit histories. Unlike prime loans, which are available at competitive market rates to people with good credit, subprime loans are offered at several percentage points above the prime interest rate to compensate lenders for the greater risk they take in making the loans.

As home prices fall and lenders impose tougher standards in response to defaults, some prime borrowers holding adjustable-rate loans are finding it difficult to refinance.

Most of the subprime loans now facing default are adjustable-rate mortgages (ARMs). Federal agencies define subprime ARMs as having one or more of the following features:

- Low initial introductory rate for a short period, which then adjusts to a variable rate several points above the prime rate for the loan's term

- No limits—or very high limits—on how much the monthly payments or interest rate can increase when the loan resets

- Little or no documentation of borrower's income required

- Substantial prepayment penalties or prepayment penalties after the introductory period

- Other features that would result in frequent refinancing to secure an affordable monthly payment

The Subprime Ripple Effect

By early 2008, more than one in five subprime mortgages was delinquent or in some stage of foreclosure. The crisis appears to be spreading beyond the subprime market.

As home prices fall and lenders impose tougher standards in response to defaults, some prime borrowers holding adjustable-rate loans are finding it difficult to refinance, which many of them had expected to be able to do before their rates reset. As defaults and foreclosures increase, investors in mortgage-backed securities also face steep losses.

How could problems with subprime mortgages, which represent a relatively narrow slice of the overall home finance market, have such a profound effect on the economy at large? The answer lies in what many observers characterize as a perfect storm of economic and market forces. While a few analysts focus on the role of one or more particular players in the mortgage meltdown, from borrowers to lenders to mortgage brokers, most attribute the crisis to a host of factors. These include but are not limited to historically cheap credit, innovations in financial products that increased the availability of subprime loans, and the rapid run-up and subsequent fall of housing prices.

If historically low interest rates and subprime loans share the blame for the housing bust, they also helped fuel the housing boom, by increasing demand for new and existing properties.

Causes of the Mortgage Meltdown

You can find the origins of the mortgage crisis in the U.S. housing bubble, which reached its peak in 2005. Historically low interest rates combined with new mortgage products that appeared to make home ownership more accessible encouraged record numbers of people to purchase and refinance homes.

Lenders competed for new business by offering attractive incentives, such as low introductory rates, reduced down payments, and interest-only loans. Many borrowers took advantage of these offers assuming that interest rates would remain low and property values would continue to increase, so that they would be able to refinance at favorable terms.

However, some borrowers did not fully understand or were not properly informed of the risks involved—for instance, that the interest rates on ARMs could rise sharply once the loans reset, dramatically increasing monthly payments. Some lenders compounded the risks inherent in these mortgage products with lax underwriting, in which borrowers were approved for loans that they had little chance of being able to repay.

Today, record numbers of homeowners are making the choice to walk away from their homes—and their mortgage payments.

If historically low interest rates and subprime loans share the blame for the housing bust, they also helped fuel the housing boom, by increasing demand for new and existing properties. According to the S&P/Case-Shiller national home-price index, the prices of homes in the U.S. rose 124% between 1997 and 2006. Aggressive lending to people with weak credit contributed to this growth. During this same period, subprime loans grew from 9% to over 20% of the mortgage market. Lending and borrowing practices based on an overly optimistic assessment of the housing market also played a role. Because the nationwide housing market hadn't suffered serious setbacks in the recent past, few anticipated that these trends would change in the future. As home prices rose, many people of all income levels took advantage of the low interest rates to refinance against the rising values of their homes, taking out cash that they used for other purchases. Many didn't anticipate that their borrowing costs could go up because interest rates might rise, or that their homes might drop in value in the future.

However, by 2006, the cost of housing had reached what it's now easy to see were unsustainable levels. This, coupled with the effects of overbuilding in many parts of the U.S., started to drive home prices downward.

With home prices dropping, some borrowers owed more on their homes than those homes were worth. Unable to refinance due to this negative equity, and with home sales slowing, unprecedented numbers of people began falling behind on their mortgage payments. Some delinquencies were the result of a rate reset. But the majority were due to borrowers who simply could not afford their loans even at the introductory rate.

Today, record numbers of homeowners are making the choice to walk away from their homes—and their mortgage payments. Some families are making that decision out of necessity. Others, overextended by investment properties or second homes, may feel little incentive to pour more money into properties that have lost value and have little chance of rebounding anytime soon.

Securitization and the Mortgage Crisis

Squeezed homeowners and lenders facing record numbers of defaults aren't the only ones affected by the mortgage crisis. Countless institutional and individual investors are also experiencing its effects, and it's reverberating throughout financial markets around the world.

At one time, mortgage lenders kept their loans on their balance sheets until they were paid off. But, in 1938, Congress created the Federal National Mortgage Association—now known as Fannie Mae—to create a secondary market for mortgages to create greater liquidity and increase the flow of capital to homeowners.

Today, quasi-government agencies, including Fannie Mae and Freddie Mac [Federal Home Loan Mortgage Corporation] and the government agency Ginnie Mae [Government National Mortgage Association] facilitate the bundling of loans into mortgage-backed securities to sell to institutional investors. Lenders use the proceeds from these sales to finance new mortgages. The government sets limits on the size and quality of the mortgages these agencies can purchase. Those that qualify—generally prime loans of under $417,000 made to borrowers whose total debt meets agency standards—are called conforming loans. . . .

More recently, investment banks began competing with the agencies in the securitization of mortgages. According to *Inside Mortgage Finance*, from 2003 to 2006, the agencies' share of mortgage-backed securities issuance fell from 76% to 43%. On the other hand, Wall Street's share of the secondary mortgage market climbed from 24% to 57% during the same period. The rapid proliferation of so-called private label issues went hand-in-hand with an equally profound change in mortgage underwriting. Fannie Mae and Freddie Mac purchase and securitize loans they acquire based on guidelines which do not allow for the purchase of many subprime loans or loans with balances above the conforming loan limit. Private label issuance was an outlet to the secondary market for many subprime and other nonconforming loans.

Collateralized Debt Obligations

Investment banks repackaged mortgages into innovative financial products that promised to boost returns for investors with little increase in risk. One widespread example is the collateralized debt obligation (CDO), which could be used to repackage mortgage-backed securities into top-rated investment-grade bonds. Here's how it worked.

1. Investment banks purchased mortgages and pooled them into mortgage-backed securities (MBS). The safest portions, or tranches, of these received the highest bond ratings of AAA/Aaa, while riskier ones received a medium-quality BBB/Bbb rating, slightly above junk bonds. Bondholders' interest was paid out of the combined mortgage payments of homeowners. Holders of the safest securities received the lowest in-

terest payments and holders of the medium-rated securities received the higher interest payments to compensate them for increased risk.

2. Financial institutions seeking new markets purchased these mortgage-backed securities. Then they pooled them with other similarly rated MBS and sometimes derivatives and issued new securities, called collateralized debt obligations (CDOs).

3. Similar to an MBS, the individual bonds for sale within each CDO were divided into several different tranches, or classes, with different interest rates and ratings. In a typical CDO, many of the bonds received the highest AAA/Aaa rating, even though they were collateralized by MBS that were in turn collaterized by subprime loans.

A smaller percentage received a BBB/Bbb rating or less. The lower-rated tranches in the CDO were designed to protect the highly rated tranches against losses. If underlying mortgages went into default, losses would affect the lowest-rated tranches first and the other tranches would not be affected until losses became more severe.

4. Some of a CDO's lower-rated tranches might have been repackaged into new CDOs.

This process of buying mortgages, creating MBS, and packaging these MBS into CDOs was designed to apportion credit risk to those parties who were willing to take it on. Instead of a lender maintaining the risk on its books, it could sell that risk to investors. It can be argued that this disassociation of risk from originators made some lenders less careful about whom they loaned money to. The elevated returns offered by MBS and CDOs arguably also made some investment firms less cautious about the creditworthiness of the loans they bought.

Meanwhile, economists point out that regulators may have been slow to respond to the developing crisis, since they assumed that securitization made the markets safer through diversification. In fact, the complex new investment products created out of subprime loans may have magnified the crisis in unforeseen ways.

Subprime Domino Effect

Many investors and analysts assumed that CDOs were diversified, and hence made less risky, due to the large number of individual bonds that might underlie a given deal. But because many collateralized debt obligations (CDOs) hold the same types of bonds, and even in some cases bonds issued by the same MBS deal, lenders and investors were not as insulated against downturns as they thought they were.

This is because the investments within the CDOs turned out to be more highly correlated than expected. That is, they performed in step with each other to an extent that was not predicted.

> *Some economists, regulators, industry members, and consumer advocates are ... recommending the creation of a unified regulatory framework and federal authority to oversee mortgage lending.*

Lenders, feeling the impact of record numbers of foreclosures, are sharply curtailing their lending. This in turn is making it all the more difficult for homeowners in all economic brackets to refinance out of adjustable-rate mortgages and other loans that are scheduled to reset at higher interest rates. Unable to sell for enough to cover their debt, some homeowners are choosing to walk away from their homes. Facing defaults even among some prime borrowers, many lenders have significantly tightened approval requirements for first-time homebuyers—even those with good credit and an adequate down payment. Some economists worry that stringent restrictions on potential homebuyers could further dampen the economy.

Meanwhile, with defaults threatening to affect all CDO tranches, not just the lowest-rated slices, the ratings agencies have been downgrading them. Many institutional investors, including international investment companies, banks, and hedge funds around the world, are facing steep losses. Some economists predict that losses are likely to add up to hundreds of billions of dollars, and could take their toll on the financial markets for years to come.

Managing the Mortgage Crisis

Financial institutions, regulators, consumer and industry advocates, and Congress are looking at a range of remedies to provide relief for homeowners, reform lending practices, and address broader systemic weaknesses in the home finance and structured finance industries.

Investment and banking industry advocates express concern that overzealous reforms could stifle financial innovation and make it harder for reputable borrowers who don't qualify for prime loans to purchase homes. Few would disagree, however, that some changes are needed to enact regulation of fraudulent lending practices and more rigorously and consistently evaluate mortgage applicants' financial readiness to borrow. Some economists, regulators, industry members, and consumer advocates are going several steps further and recommending the creation of a unified regulatory framework and federal authority to oversee mortgage lending. Currently, many lenders and brokers are regulated by the states, where the effectiveness and extent of enforcement varies.

In addition, some are advocating regulatory changes to bring greater transparency to the structured finance industry that creates CDOs and other complex debt securities and the over-the-counter (OTC) markets on which they trade.

In the meantime, the government has moved forward on a few initiatives to ease the credit crunch, stimulate the economy, and stem the tide of foreclosures.

The Federal Reserve has significantly lowered interest rates to create more liquidity in the market and bolster the economy. Lower interest rates may also renew interest in the housing market, while providing some relief for current homeowners whose ARMs are scheduled to reset.

The Fed, the FDIC [Federal Deposit Insurance Corporation], and other government agencies have proposed tougher guidelines and regulations to curb abusive lending practices.

The economic stimulus plan, approved by Congress in early 2008, temporarily raises the limits on the size of conforming loans from $417,000 to a maximum of $729,750. This move is designed to make it easier to qualify for large loans at prime rates and also relieve pressure in the market for jumbo mortgages. The plan also temporarily raises the limits on Federal Housing Administration (FHA) insured loans for homebuyers who qualify for this assistance.

In late 2007, the House [of Representatives] passed the Mortgage Reform and Anti-Predatory Lending Act to reform consumer mortgage practices, establish licensing and registration requirements for residential mortgage lenders, and provide minimum standards for mortgage loans. In addition, the House voted to reform the Federal Housing Administration and direct up to $300 million a year into an affordable housing fund. The Senate has yet to vote on a similar bill.

In addition, the Bush administration launched a voluntary private-sector plan called the Hope Now Alliance, which is a coordinated effort to improve outreach to borrowers and reduce the numbers who enter foreclosure. Additionally, the alliance announced a plan whereby servicers may agree to defer foreclosures for 30 days to give homeowners an opportunity to renegotiate their loans. While some applaud these programs, others counter that they are too narrowly focused to provide relief for the great majority of homeowners facing foreclosure.

Congress is considering amending the bankruptcy code to enable bankruptcy judges to write down the principal value of mortgages. Currently principal residences are exempt from re-structuring plans in bankruptcy proceedings. Such a move, proponents argue, would keep many people out of foreclosure and would limit investment losses. However, there is significant opposition to this approach. One of the chief arguments is that subjecting mortgages to involuntary write-down could drive up consumers' borrowing costs for all mortgages.

2

The Subprime Mortgage Crisis Is Destroying Homes and Neighborhoods

Jeff Swicord

Jeff Swicord writes for Voice of America, an international broadcasting service funded by the U.S. government.

Thousands of Americans have lost their homes as a result of the subprime mortgage crisis, and others have seen the value of their homes and neighborhoods deteriorate as their neighbors have been forced to abandon their homes. Cleveland has been especially hard hit. Subprime or adjustable-rate mortgages were targeted at lower income borrowers in Cleveland who could not afford traditional mortgages. Some analysts estimate that homeowners will be walking away from loans they can no longer afford through 2010 and beyond, with no sign that the subprime problem will be resolved in the near future.

The subprime mortgage crisis in the United States has rattled financial markets around the world. The crisis has triggered home foreclosures across the country, causing thousands of Americans to lose their homes, devastating entire communities. . . .

"I have things that are going to my friends. . ." says Karen Lucas, who has owned a house near Cleveland, Ohio, for 35

Jeff Swicord, "Human, Community Costs Add to Subprime Mortgage Crisis" (Part 1), *Voice of America*, March 18, 2008. "Subprime Mortgage Crisis Devastates Cleveland Neighborhoods" (Part 2), *Voice of America*, March 18, 2008. "Thousands of Subprime Borrowers Seek Financial Relief" (Part 3), *Voice of America*, March 19, 2008. Reproduced by permission.

years. The Cuyahoga County Sheriff's Office was coming the next day to serve her with foreclosure papers and force her to move.

Subprime mortgage lenders set up shop in the Cleveland area. Many people refinanced their mortgages to take advantage of historically low interest rates, and their problems began.

"We had to refinance because of my husband's company being purchased by another company. So, we refinanced, and he did lose his job from that company," she recalls.

Thousands Have Lost Their Homes

Like almost 70,000 other families in the Cleveland area over last five years, Lucas and her husband were not able to keep up with the ballooning payments of their subprime mortgage.

Going through her house she points out improvement projects she had planned, such as a kitchen renovation.

Lucas had been fighting a four-year legal battle to keep her house. She filed a final appeal with the court in an effort to hold off foreclosure for another 30 days. With hours to go, there was no word from the court.

The loans are often sold multiple times among banks, making it difficult for borrowers to keep track of who owns their loan.

"I've done my crying," she said. "I've made my peace, and I put it in God's hands."

Cleveland, Ohio, was one of America's great industrial cities of the 20th century, a heavy manufacturing town nestled along the banks of Lake Erie. Ohio has lost more than 200,000 manufacturing jobs [since 1998], and the median income in the state has declined by 10 percent.

In the late '90s, subprime mortgage lenders set up shop in the Cleveland area. Many people refinanced their mortgages to take advantage of historically low interest rates, and their problems began.

"Sometimes the house [mortgage] would be flipped [resold] to another company, and we didn't even know," says community activist Barbara Anderson. "We would still be sending the payment to the old company, and then we would get a call that would say, 'Hey, you didn't pay us.' And we would say, 'Who are you?' 'Well, we are your new [mortgage company].'"

Loans with Surprises

Subprime loans are higher interest rate loans that lenders offer to buyers who do not qualify for lower, prime rate loans. The loans are often sold multiple times among banks, making it difficult for borrowers to keep track of who owns their loan. Anderson's loan agreement contained clauses that allowed her loan servicer to add on additional fees. "'Future late fees,' I don't know what that is but that was tacked on there," she explains. "And then other fees, those were never outlined, that was tacked on there."

Her initial seven percent loan was now close to 20 percent.

With the help of a community organization that works to get people out of bad loans, the Andersons refinanced their loan at a fixed rate of 5.75 percent with a bank that does not sell its loans. Barbara Anderson is one of the lucky ones. Cuyahoga County expects more than 20,000 foreclosures [by 2009].

On the day the sheriff was scheduled to serve foreclosure papers, Karen Lucas had no word from the court about her appeal. As she sat down to talk with VOA [Voice of America], there was a knock at the door.

The visitor was an officer who was serving Lucas with the foreclosure papers. She was ordered to vacate the premises immediately. She went inside to work out the details of her move. Later, she came out to talk to VOA one last time, holding the judge's decision on her failed appeal.

"This is not justice!" she said. "They are protecting their own, and I am tired of it, tired of it!" Holding the envelope, she said, "You should read this."

It is a scene that will be duplicated thousands of times in cities across the U.S. over the next several years as the effect of the subprime loan crisis ripples across the country. Families uprooted, lives altered, memories left behind.

A Nationwide Problem

The subprime mortgage crisis has devastated property values and the quality of life in cities across the United States. . . .

"Every red dot represents a foreclosure in Cleveland," says Cuyahoga County Treasurer Jim Rokakis [as he points to a map]. He says he is feeling the weight of the collapsing subprime mortgage market in Cleveland, Ohio. "As you can see, there are some neighborhoods that literally on every block, you don't have one foreclosure, you have got 20–30 per block," Rokakis said.

When a house is foreclosed and vacated in Cleveland, within days, sometimes hours, so-called "scrappers" start ripping the aluminum siding off the house.

In [recent] years, Rokakis has seen homeowner equity erased, and entire neighborhoods destroyed, by more than 70,000 home foreclosures across the county.

"What if you are that house in the middle there?" asks Rokakis. "You're not going to sell your house. This is just between 2000 and mid-2007."

Now the county property-tax base that pays for schools, roads and other community services is under assault. In 2002, the Ohio cities of Cleveland, Dayton and Toledo passed local ordinances requiring financial counseling for people applying for subprime mortgages. Rokakis says that within two months, the banking industry convinced state lawmakers to approve legislation to override the ordinances.

Neighborhoods In Crisis

Community activist Barbara Anderson knows first hand what housing foreclosures do to a neighborhood. When a house is foreclosed and vacated in Cleveland, within days, sometimes hours, so-called "scrappers" start ripping the aluminum siding off the house. The price for scrap metal in China and India is at an all-time high. Anything metal can be sold on the international market. She points out one house where posts were taken from the first floor of a porch, and the second floor fell in.

"This doesn't look like people officially moved out. This looks like people just got up and left this house and left everything here, and then other people came and just destroyed it," Anderson said.

The scrappers break into the houses, break through the drywall and rip out the water pipes. Copper wiring and aluminum conduit are ripped out of the ceiling. Metal sinks and appliances are hauled away and sold. What was a foreclosed home in a depressed neighborhood now becomes an empty, worthless shell with little to no value.

Rokakis says the real victims are the homeowners who are able to keep their home. "You know who the real victims are? I'll tell you who the real victims are. The real victims are people in neighborhoods throughout Cleveland and the suburbs who played by the rules," he says. "They paid their taxes, they maintained their property, and they woke up one day about six years ago and there was vacant property next to them. And then they woke up a month later and there was one across the street. And another month later, there was another one down the block. Their properties, their entire life savings are tied up in their own home. That is gone. That equity is gone because the house can't be sold!"

For now, Anderson and her neighbors must live next to the aftermath. Jim Rokakis says it will take years if not decades to bring many of Cleveland's neighborhoods back to life.

Subprime, or higher interest rate, loans first appeared in Cleveland's inner-city neighborhoods. They are aimed at lower income borrowers who do not qualify for lower interest rate loans.

Help for Subprime Victims

New clients attend a gathering at the East Side Organizing Project, or ESOP, in Cleveland, Ohio. ESOP is a nonprofit community organization that works to refinance subprime mortgage borrowers on the verge of default or foreclosure. Project director James Jones oversees three orientation sessions a week. He recollects attendance at previous orientation sessions.

"Back in August [2007] we were having 20 to 25 people in a session. And that went on for about a month and a half. It seemed like it cooled down a bit. In October it exploded again," he said.

Jones says subprime, or higher interest rate, loans first appeared in Cleveland's inner-city neighborhoods. They are aimed at lower income borrowers who do not qualify for lower interest loans. Low adjustable-rate mortgages, or ARMs, benefit first-time buyers because of the loans' introductory rates. But those rates usually increase in two to five years.

"Some of those folks may have fallen victim. When they sat down to read the contract, they saw that it had a variable rate and they may have asked the broker, 'What does that mean?'" Jones said.

Buyers Left Holding the Bag

He explains, by the time the mortgages ballooned, the broker had closed up shop and left the area. And the borrower was left with a mortgage that he or she could no longer afford.

Mark Trawicki says he fell victim to a fast-talking broker.

"Well, he looked over my original loan, and he said, 'I can reduce your monthly payment by about a hundred bucks.' And I said, 'OK, that sounds like a good deal,' and it would be an adjustable rate for five years," he explained.

His mortgage ballooned from 3.7 percent to 8.25 percent, and he says he is having trouble paying his bills.

"So, at this point I am trying to stop the hemorrhaging and get back to something I can work with," he said.

ESOP counselor Kristin Anderson says Trawicki's financial situation is better than most clients. She will try to get his lender to renegotiate his mortgage to a more affordable fixed rate.

"He is showing a surplus in his income," she noted. "So, they might say that he can afford this. So usually, I go back and fight with the lender and say if you don't put him into a fixed rate, eventually he is not going to be able to pay his mortgage."

East Side Organizing Project officers say they do not expect foreclosures in the Cleveland area to slow down anytime soon. They say more homeowners will be walking through their door looking for help well beyond 2010.

3

Disregard for Applicants' Incomes Contributed to the Subprime Problem

Gretchen Morgenson

Gretchen Morgenson is a Pulitzer Prize–winning journalist who writes the "Market Watch" column for the Sunday New York Times.

The subprime crisis was caused in part by dishonesty on the part of loan applicants, who lied in order to get loans they could not afford. However, lenders had a tool, form 4506T, that would have allowed them to verify borrowers' income information with the Internal Revenue Service. Overwhelmingly, lenders did not take advantage of this safeguard. They made representations and warranties to investors about the quality of the loans they made, yet failed to exercise due diligence in verifying the information. For this reason, they may be liable for damage, should investors decide to pursue their claims in court.

W e've all heard a great deal in recent months about the greedy borrowers who caused the subprime mortgage calamity. Hordes of them duped unsuspecting lenders, don't you know, by falsifying their incomes on loan documents. Now those loans are in default and the rapacious borrowers have moved on with their riches.

People who make these claims, with a straight face no less, overlook a crucial fact. Almost all mortgage applicants had to sign a document allowing lenders to verify their incomes with the Internal Revenue Service [I.R.S.]. At least 90 percent of borrowers had to sign, seal and deliver this form, known as a 4506T, industry experts say. This includes the so-called stated income mortgages, affectionately known as "liar loans."

So while borrowers may have misrepresented their incomes, either on their own or at the urging of their mortgage brokers, lenders had the tools to identify these fibs before making the loans. All they had to do was ask the I.R.S. The fact that in most cases they apparently didn't do so puts the lie to the idea that cagey borrowers duped unsuspecting lenders to secure on loans that are now—surprise!—failing.

Instead, lenders appear to be complicit in the rampant fibbery that is one of the root causes of our continuing mortgage nightmare.

Don't Ask, Don't Tell

Mike Summers, vice president for sales and marketing at Veritax Inc., in Tustin, Calif., knows plenty about this. His company handles the filing of these verification forms with the I.R.S. on behalf of lenders and loan originators. He began selling the service to lenders in 1999 and said he was surprised at the reaction he received—like that of a skunk at a garden party.

"In 2001, I was going around the subprime world trying to get them to sign up," Mr. Summers recalled. "Ameriquest, and others I don't want to name, just didn't want to know because it would kill the deals. The attitude was don't ask, don't tell."

Ameriquest, just to jog your memory, is now defunct.

Mr. Summers said Ameriquest and other prospective clients used lame reasons for turning him down. Submitting the forms was too costly, they said ($20 per loan, on average), or too time-consuming (the information came back to the lender in about one business day).

"It was greed on a few different levels," Mr. Summers said. "I don't think $20 to protect your interest in a $500,000 loan and weed out things that aren't going to work is that big an investment."

In 2006, the I.R.S. made it even easier for lenders to verify borrowers' incomes by automating its systems, Mr. Summers said. The turnaround time under the new system fell significantly.

Still, the tool remained unused. When a customer signed up for Veri-tax's service, it was typically to spot-check the quality of loans after they were made, Mr. Summers said.

Forty-three percent of the cases sampled in the study [of suspected mortgage fraud] involved misrepresentation of income, assets or debts.

"My estimate was between 3 and 5 percent of all the loans that were funded in 2006 were executed with a 4506," Mr. Summers said. "They just turned a blind eye, saying, 'Everything is going to be fine.'"

We know how well that turned out. Lenders still do not routinely check borrowers' incomes with the I.R.S., Mr. Summers said. This seems odd, given how easy it is to hop onto the Internet and create documents that look like authentic W-2s or Form 1040s.

Indeed, according to a report on mortgage fraud released . . . [in April 2008] by the Financial Crimes Enforcement Network, a unit of the Treasury Department, only 31 percent of suspected fraud was detected before loan disbursements in the 12 months ended March 31, 2007. On stated income loans, only 19 percent of the cases of suspected fraud were detected before the loans were financed, versus 33.5 percent on more fully documented loans.

Yet 43 percent of the cases sampled in the study involved misrepresentation of income, assets or debts. The next-largest category was forged documents, totaling 28 percent of the sampled loans.

It Was Easy to Lie About Income

Mortgage brokers initiated the loans on 64 percent of the reports involving misrepresentation of income, assets or debt, the study said.

The study's findings on the institutions that file suspicious-activity reports related to mortgages are also revealing. Banks, of course, file a vast majority of these reports. Securities firms, which packaged and sold billions of dollars in mortgage loans to investors and were certainly in a position to identify problems in them, filed almost none. They seemed to have little appetite for the job.

Given that many of these lenders are out of business, ultimately this could come back to the bank or investment bank.

During the 12 months ended March 31, 2007, banks filed 41,000 reports on suspected mortgage fraud. By comparison, during the more than four years that ended May 1 of [2007], 18 securities firms filed just 36 reports of suspicious activity.

The degree to which mortgage lenders and Wall Street looked the other way on borrowers' incomes, a sin of commission given the ease with which they could have been checked, raises an intriguing question.

Can investors stuck with losses on these loans sue to recover their investments based on this due-diligence failure? After all, mortgage originators made representations and warranties to investors that the quality of these loans was good when it clearly was not. And they made these representations knowing that they had not bothered to conduct quick and easy borrower-income checks.

"Investors hoping to put back the loans for deficient underwriting under reps and warranties would end up going back to the originators," said Josh Rosner, an analyst at Graham Fisher & Company and an authority on mortgage-backed securities. "Given that many of these lenders are out of business, ultimately this could come back to the bank or investment bank."

"The general view is this should not be talked about out loud," Mr. Rosner added.

Wall Street will certainly battle forcefully against such lawsuits, if investors bring them. But its role as one of the great enablers in this mortgage debacle is something that even Wall Street can't deny.

4

Wall Street Created the Subprime Problem

Paul Muolo

Paul Muolo is executive editor of National Mortgage News *and* Mortgage Servicing News. *He writes a column, "Mortgage Scene," that appears regularly on MSN.*

Hundreds of mortgage banking firms have closed since December 2006, and thousands of jobs have been lost. Loan volumes are shrinking as prospective home buyers, worried about the economy and the possibility of losing value on their investment, are not proceeding with their plans to buy new homes. Responsibility for this crisis lies with the Wall Street investment community. Wall Street created the market for subprime loans and found the investors, but failed to do due diligence, to assure that buyers had the means to pay for the mortgages they took out. Now Wall Street holds $210 billion in subprime receivables that probably cannot be collected.

President Harry Truman had a sign on his desk that said, "The Buck Stops Here." The legendary phrase is still part of the American lexicon, even though 60 years have passed and few of our civic and business leaders step up to the plate when it comes to taking responsibility for financial and political disasters.

As every mortgage executive knows, the business of lending money to consumers in the throes of a disaster—at least it certainly feels like a disaster: 200 mortgage banking firms and platforms have closed since December of 2006, 30,000 jobs were lost in August [2007] and 30,000 more likely will disappear [by the end of 2007], probably more.

Loan volumes are waning and the consumer is spooked. Even though the U.S. unemployment picture looks good, homebuyers are afraid to sign on the dotted line because they believe (and rightfully so) that the house they covet can be purchased more cheaply if they just wait a month or two.

Predicting a bottom in this industry is never easy but chances are the market won't begin to recover until late [2008]. As professionals begin to gather for the annual MBA [Master of Business Administration] convention in Boston, there will be plenty of job seekers roaming the trade show floor. I wish them luck.

Sherri Markel, a Florida loan broker, recently wrote to me, detailing the dismal state of the mortgage business there. Commenting on the Florida job market for brokers and LOs [loan originators], she wrote: "Even with my three to five years of mortgage industry experience and post-license-credited training, the chances of me being the candidate getting the job offer" is "about the same as hitting the lottery."

Wall Street created the loan programs marketed by loan brokers and mortgage bankers.

There are two mortgage markets out there right now, the conventional/government segment . . . and the nonprime sector, which is currently on life support. It boils down to this: if a mortgage customer has good credit they have nothing to worry about. Yes, the jumbo market is still a little dicey but loans are still being funded. The consumer may have to pay more but at least they can get a loan.

The $150 Billion Price Tag

Then there's subprime land. It's not pretty. You've read the articles in *National Mortgage News*, *American Banker*, and other trade publications. The story has now become big enough that the general media and networks are finally paying attention. The price tag is at $150 billion and counting. Consumers are going to lose their homes and equity, and investors in subprime bonds have already lost billions. How did this happen?

The answer lies at the top: Wall Street. In the subprime sector the buck stops at the doors of Bear Stearns, Merrill Lynch, Lehman Bros., Normura [investment banks]—take your pick. Will the executives at these firms take responsibility for the subprime mess?

This is what happened: Wall Street created the loan programs marketed by loan brokers and mortgage bankers. The mortgages were funded by non-depository wholesalers like Acoustic Home Loans, Mortgage Lenders Network, New Century, Ownit Mortgage (fill in the blank).

Firms like Bear [Stearns] and Merrill [Lynch] thought they could buy billions in loans without doing much in the way of due diligence on the loan files.

Not only did the Street create the programs and buy the end-product (mortgages), they financed many of the same non-depositories they were purchasing loans from. These warehouse lines of credit and "gestation repos" were extended liberally. In 2004, when the subprime market took off in earnest, Wall Street wasn't exactly asking for much in the way of financial ID—they were looking for volume.

And volume they got. In 2005, subprime production soared to a record $795 billion, accounting for almost one in every four mortgages funded that year. Ten years earlier subprime lenders originated just $35 billion (that's not a typo), accounting for 5.5% of all loans originated.

Wall Street Profited from a Bad Situation

Why did blueblood Street firms such as Merrill Lynch—known for peddling stocks to America's wealthy—go gaga for subprime? Answer: because they saw gold in the hills of housing finance. They also saw that Fannie and Freddie [government mortgage markets] were too busy licking their accounting wounds to compete against the Street in the nonprime market.

But Wall Street badly calculated, which is what happens when people who think they're smarter than everyone else enter a business. Street firms like Bear and Merrill thought they could buy billions in loans without doing much in the way of due diligence on the loan files. (Note: this doesn't absolve sleazy loan brokers, AEs [account executives], the rating agencies and house "flippers" for their shortcomings either. But that's a column for a future time.)

Steve Halper, CEO of DataVerify, a software firm, said his company demonstrated its fraud prevention system "to every investor (including Merrill) on Wall Street. Their response was that they were making too much money to slow down the golden pipeline for any silly fraud tool."

I've heard the same story from several other industry executives. It's not just sour grapes from a vendor scorned. One insider from a large West Coast correspondent buyer recently relayed a story about how his company approached a subprime wholesaler about buying more of its loan production.

The loan buyer, however, wanted to review 80% of the loan files they were purchasing. An executive at the wholesaler (name withheld to protect the source of the story) told the West Coast loan buyer that Bear Stearns was buying his production but was only reviewing 20% of the loan files. As you might guess, the West Coast loan buyer didn't get the account.

Wall Street played a larger role in the subprime industry than just banking and buying loans. Two years ago, some firms (Merrill, others) began acquiring subprime lending shops as a way to assure a steady flow of production. I would venture that all the heads rolling in the mortgage departments on Wall Street these days are a result of either those acquisitions or a lack of due diligence on loan purchases.

Will Wall Street run screaming from the subprime industry, red ink oozing from their pores? They already are. I just hope the door doesn't hit them in the bum on the way out. Street firms have amassed $210 billion in subprime receivables (servicing rights), or 18% of the market. I wish them luck with that.

5

Washington Is Responsible for the Subprime Crisis

John Atlas and Peter Dreier

John Atlas is president of the National Housing Institute (NHI), a nonprofit research and policy center that sponsors Shelterforce *magazine. Peter Dreier is professor of politics and director of the Urban & Environmental Policy Program at Occidental College in Los Angeles, and coauthor of* The Next Los Angeles: The Struggle for a Livable City.

The blame for the subprime crisis goes to the conservatives within the White House and Congress who have spent decades working to eliminate government regulation within the lending industry. During the period after the Great Depression, the savings-and-loan industry was highly regulated by the federal government. By the early 1980s, Congress began to hold back. Since then, the industry has been in a downward spiral. The free market ideologies of conservatives in Washington are at the heart of the crisis.

Since 1998, more than 7 million borrowers bought homes with sub-prime loans. One million of those homeowners have already defaulted on their loans. The crisis is likely to get worse. Financial analysts predict that at least a quarter of these people—over 2 million families—will default and face the financial pain and psychological grief of losing their homes over the next few years.

Bush, who once touted his administration's goal as creating an "ownership society," may now go down in history as

John Atlas and Peter Dreier, "The Conservative Origins of the Sub-Prime Mortgage Crisis," *The American Prospect*, December 18, 2007.

the president on whose watch ownership declined. The nation's homeownership rate has fallen during the last two years and will plummet further next year. Moreover, Bush's unwillingness to take bold steps to regulate lenders, brokers, and investors will guarantee that the next president will inherit a much bigger mortgage mess.

To many Americans, the crisis seems too complex to comprehend. To understand it, we need to know: What is the problem? Who benefited? Who got hurt? Who is to blame? Who should we help? What should be done? Although the immediate cause is the widespread use of sub-prime mortgages, the root cause is a decades-old failure of government to adequately regulate the banking industry.

It All Started with Deregulation

There was a time, not too long ago, when Washington did regulate banks. The Depression triggered the creation of government bank regulations and agencies, such as the Federal Deposit Insurance Corporation, the Federal Home Loan Bank System, Homeowners Loan Corporation, Fannie Mae, and the Federal Housing Administration, to protect consumers and expand homeownership. After World War II, until the late 1970s, the system worked. The savings-and-loan industry was highly regulated by the federal government, with a mission to take people's deposits and then provide loans for the sole purpose of helping people buy homes to live in. Washington insured those loans through the FDIC, provided mortgage discounts through FHA and the Veterans Administration, created a secondary mortgage market to guarantee a steady flow of capital, and required S&Ls [savings and loan associations] to make predictable 30-year fixed loans. The result was a steady increase in homeownership and few foreclosures.

In the 1970s, when community groups discovered that lenders and the FHA were engaged in systematic racial discrimination against minority consumers and neighborhoods—a practice called "redlining"—they mobilized and got Congress, led by Wisconsin Senator William Proxmire, to adopt the Community Reinvestment Act and the Home Mortgage Disclosure Act, which together have significantly reduced racial disparities in lending.

The deregulation of banking led to merger mania, with banks and S&Ls gobbling each other up and making loans to finance shopping malls, golf courses, office buildings, and condo projects that had no financial logic other than a quick-buck profit.

But by the early 1980s, the lending industry used its political clout to push back against government regulation. In 1980, Congress adopted the Depository Institutions Deregulatory and Monetary Control Act, which eliminated interest-rate caps and made sub-prime lending more feasible for lenders. The S&Ls balked at constraints on their ability to compete with conventional banks engaged in commercial lending. They got Congress—Democrats and Republicans alike—to change the rules, allowing S&Ls to begin a decade-long orgy of real estate speculation, mismanagement, and fraud. The poster child for this era was Charles Keating, who used his political connections and donations to turn a small Arizona S&L into a major real estate speculator, snaring five Senators (the so-called "Keating Five," including John McCain) into his web of corruption.

The deregulation of banking led to merger mania, with banks and S&Ls gobbling each other up and making loans to finance shopping malls, golf courses, office buildings, and condo projects that had no financial logic other than a quick-buck profit. When the dust settled in the late 1980s, hundreds of S&Ls and banks had gone under, billions of dollars of commercial loans were useless, and the federal government was left to bail out the depositors whose money the speculators had put at risk.

[Free market ideologists] believe that government is always the problem, never the solution, and that regulation of private business is always bad.

The stable neighborhood S&L soon became a thing of the past. Banks, insurance companies, credit card firms and other money-lenders were now part of a giant "financial services" industry, while Washington walked away from its responsibility to protect consumers with rules, regulations, and enforcement. Meanwhile, starting with [President Ronald] Reagan, the federal government slashed funding for low-income housing, and allowed the FHA [Federal Housing Administration], once a key player helping working-class families purchase a home, to drift into irrelevancy.

Into this vacuum stepped banks, mortgage lenders, and scam artists, looking for ways to make big profits from consumers desperate for the American Dream of homeownership. They invented new "loan products" that put borrowers at risk. Thus was born the sub-prime market.

To Conservatives, Free Market Is the Answer, Not Government

At the heart of the crisis are the conservative free market ideologists whose views increasingly influenced American politics since the 1980s, and who still dominate the Bush administration. They believe that government is always the problem, never the solution, and that regulation of private business is always bad. Lenders and brokers who fell outside of federal regulations made most of the sub-prime and predatory loans.

In 2000, Edward M. Gramlich, a Federal Reserve Board member, repeatedly warned about sub-prime mortgages and predatory lending, which he said "jeopardize the twin American dreams of owning a home and building wealth." He tried to get [Federal Reserve Board] chairman Alan Greenspan to crack down on irrational sub-prime lending by increasing oversight, but his warnings fell on deaf ears, including those in Congress.

As Rep. Barney Frank wrote recently in *The Boston Globe*, the surge of sub-prime lending was a sort of "natural experiment" testing the theories of those who favor radical deregulation of financial markets. And the lessons, Frank said, are clear: "To the extent that the system did work, it is because of prudential regulation and oversight. Where it was absent, the result was tragedy."

American's Moods Are Shifting

Some political observers believe that the American mood is shifting, finally recognizing that the frenzy of deregulation that began in the 1980s has triggered economic chaos and declining living standards. If they needed proof, the foreclosure crisis is exhibit number one.

Those who profited handsomely from the sub-prime market and predatory lending, the mortgage bankers and brokers, are working overtime to protect their profits by lobbying in state capitals and in Washington, DC to keep government off their backs. The banking industry, of course, has repeatedly warned that any restrictions on their behavior will close needy people out of the home-buying market. Its lobbyists insisted that the Bush plan be completely voluntary.

This isn't surprising, considering who was at the negotiating table when the Bush administration, led by Treasury Secretary Henry Paulson, forged the plan. The key players were the mortgage service companies (who collect the homeowner's monthly payments, or foreclose when they fall behind) and groups representing investors holding the mortgages, dominated by Wall Street banks. The Bush plan reflected both groups' calculation that—for some loans—they would do better temporarily freezing interest rates than foreclosing. Groups who represent consumers—ACORN [Association of Community Organizations for Reform Now], the National Community Reinvestment Coalition, the Greenlining Institute, Neighborhood Housing Services, and the Center for Responsible Lending—were not invited to the negotiation.

The best hope for real reform rests with a Democratic Party victory in November. And after an electoral win, it will require that Democrats make sure that these consumer groups are key participants in shaping legislation. And wouldn't it be nice to hear the next president tell the American people that, "the era of unregulated so-called free-market banking greed and sleaze is over"?

The Federal Reserve Board Is Responsible for the Subprime Crisis

Tito Boeri and Luigi Guiso

Tito Boeri is a professor of economics at Bocconi University in Milan, Italy. His field of research is labor economics, redistributive policies, and political economics. Luigi Guiso is a professor of economics at the European University Institute in Florence, Italy. His research interests include households' savings and financial decisions, firms' investment and adjustment policies, and culture and economic performance.

The subprime crisis has three causes: The inadequate financial knowledge of U.S. households, a financial innovation called "securitization" that allowed the bundling together of massive mortgage portfolios which could then be sold to investors, and the fiscal policies of former Federal Reserve Board Chairman Alan Greenspan. Greenspan bears the greatest share of responsibility. After September 11, 2001, Greenspan lowered interest rates dramatically, flooding the economic system with cash. Lenders began extending credit to people who were not credit worthy.

> The subprime crisis has its origin in [Alan] Greenspan's low interest rate policy. His successor [the new Federal Reserve Board chairman] should take care to reassure the markets in the short run without laying the foundations for a new overreaction "à la Greenspan."

It's difficult to predict how long the crisis in the world's financial markets will last. Its dynamics recalls that of previous crises, . . . which have by now been forgotten by many. An excess of liquidity (i.e. an abundance of loans at low cost) has suddenly been transformed into a dearth of liquidity; many dealers find it hard to sell the assets in their portfolios. The present crisis bears little resemblance to the 1929 Great Depression, contrary to what some politicians and commentators assert. Fortunately Fed [Federal Reserve] President Ben Bernanke has studied the Great Depression in depth. According to the analysis he did as an academic, the "Great Depression" was unleashed by a collapse of production and consumption, amplified by a drastic reduction in the supply of bank credit which came about largely because the Fed failed to act as a lender of last resort. Exactly the opposite is happening today. The world economy continues to grow at sustained rates since central banks have so far fulfilled their roles of supplying the necessary liquidity to the market. The only . . . aspect that the current crisis shares with the Great Depression is that its epicenter is the U.S.

The Present Financial Crisis

It's useful to disentangle the causes of the crisis. Three factors contribute to the current crisis that was triggered by the expectation of defaults on subprime mortgages in the U.S.:

- The low financial literacy of U.S. households;

- The financial innovation that has resulted in the massive securitisation of illiquid assets, and;

- The low interest rate policy followed by Alan Greenspan's Fed from 2001 to 2004.

The third cause is by far the most important. Without Greenspan's policy, the present crisis probably would have never occurred.

The first ingredient of the crisis is a blend of bad information, financial inexperience and myopia of consumers/ investors. They fell for the prospect of getting a mortgage at rates never seen before and then extrapolating these rates out for thirty years. This myopia was encouraged and indeed exploited by banks and other lenders eager to attract and retain clients. This is surprisingly similar to what has been seen in the past when banks and intermediaries have advised their clients to invest in financial assets ill-suited to their ability to bear risk. In both cases, a biased advisor is the reflection of a clear conflict of interest in the financial industry. Financial literacy is low not only in financially backward countries (as one would expect), but also in the U.S. Only two out of three Americans are familiar with the law of compound interest; less than half know how to measure the effects of inflation on the costs of indebtedness. Financial literacy is particularly low among those who have taken out subprime mortgages. The intermediaries exploited this financial illiteracy.

The monetary policy of low interest rates . . . injected an enormous amount of liquidity into the global monetary system.

Securitisation and Low Interest Rates

The second ingredient is the pace of financial innovation during the last ten years and the securitisation that it produced. Today it is easy to "liquidify" a portfolio of illiquid credits (typically a combination of bank loans or mortgages) so they can be packaged into investor portfolios. Any bank with distressed loans has used this technique to securitise its own credits. Like all financial innovations, this too has pros and cons. The advantage is that by making an illiquid credit liquid, one can achieve important efficiency gains; investors can take longer-term positions and so earn a higher return. It also spreads the risk of insolvency across a much wider group, reducing the level of risk exposure of any individual agent. But securitisations also have their disadvantages. They weaken the incentives of financial intermediaries to monitor the behavior of the original borrower. In addition, since a credit that has become risky can be liquidated more easily, banks have less incentive to screen borrowers carefully. This opens the credit-markets doors to poor quality borrowers.

Thanks Alan! Today we're paying the cost of your overre-action to the 2001 recession.

The first two factors aren't new. Without the third factor—the legacy of the "central banker of the century"—the crisis probably would have never occurred. The monetary policy of low interest rates—introduced by Alan Greenspan in response to the post-9/11 recession and the collapse of the new economy "bubble"—injected an enormous amount of liquidity into the global monetary system. This reduced short-term interest rates to 1%—their lowest level in 50 years. What's more, Greenspan spent the next two years maintaining interest rates at levels significantly below equilibrium. Interest rates were kept at low levels for a long time, and were often negative in inflation-adjusted terms. The result was no surprise. Low returns on traditional investments pushed investors and lenders to take bigger risks to get better returns. Financial intermediaries, in search of profits, extended credit to families and companies with limited financial strength. Investors with varying degrees of expertise duly reallocated their portfolios towards more lucrative but riskier assets in an attempt to increase their wealth and preserve its purchasing power. The low borrowing rates for both short- and long-term maturity attracted throngs of borrowers—families above all who were se-duced by the possibility of acquiring assets that had always been beyond their means. At the same time, house prices soared, ultimately encouraging the additional extension of credit; the value of real estate seemed almost guaranteed.

We Must Prevent a Future Crisis

Thanks Alan! Today we're paying the cost of your overreaction to the 2001 recession. The ECB [European Central Bank] was wisely prudent and only let itself be partially tempted by Keynesian [British economist John Maynard Keynes proposed solutions to twentieth-century depressions in Britain and the U.S.] arguments for reduced interest rates (which were already absurdly low) as a tool for attacking European stagnation. Many would like the ECB to lower rates now, arguing that to avoid a new "Great Depression" Europe needs Keynesian policy of the type followed in the U.S.A., Great Britain and Germany after the 1929 collapse.

We think it is far better to avoid repeating Greenspan's error, and to avoid monetary policies that are too accommodating for too long. At present, central banks are acting correctly by injecting liquidity into the system. In such crises, one must be afraid of fear. Expectations can unleash downward spirals that make the most pessimistic prophecies come true. In addition, the market crisis hits everyone indiscriminately—even those who did not make money by extending mortgages too readily. Last Friday's press release of the Federal Open Market Committee didn't clarify whether half-point cut in the discount rate as intended to merely prevent a downward expectations spiral or whether it was the prelude to yet another overreaction to the market crisis. It's important to show soon that the lesson of Greenspan's error has been learned. We should not overreact, as has been done so may times in the past, by sowing the seeds of a future crisis today.

7

The Federal Reserve Board Is Not Responsible for the Subprime Crisis

Irwin M. Stelzer

Irwin M. Stelzer is a contributing editor to the Weekly Standard *and director of economic policy studies at the Hudson Institute. He is also a columnist for the* Sunday Times *of London.*

Some critics have blamed former Federal Reserve Board Chairman Alan Greenspan for volatility in the stock market, the tightening of credit markets in 2007, and other economic events that are related to the collapse of the subprime mortgage market. They point to a statement Greenspan made in 2004, to the effect that borrowers could potentially benefit from a variety of loan products, including the adjustable-rate mortgages (ARMs) that are implicated in the recent housing crisis. However, Greenspan is not to blame. Rather, mortgage brokers arranged loans for many people who otherwise would not have been able to afford homes, using ARMs as a tool. Sometimes brokers did not advise their customers about the risks of ARMs.

Washington pundits are not famous for their kindness to politicians, regulators, and other out-of-power figures to whom they no longer crave access. So it should come as no surprise that Alan Greenspan [the former chairman of the Federal Reserve Board] has been nominated as the culprit [of billion-dollar investor losses], and that the process of chipping away at the pedestal on which he stands has begun.

It seems that the recent volatility in share prices, the tightening of credit that has made several proposed private equity deals uneconomic, the collapse of the subprime mortgage market and with it several hedge funds, and the decision by Wells Fargo to raise its interest on 30-year fixed mortgages in excess of $400,000, are due to—you guessed it—the former chairman of the Federal Reserve Board.

Sub-prime borrowers were encouraged to take out adjustable rate mortgages (ARMs), many of which are now in default as a result of higher interest rates.

The Truth About the Non-prime Mortgage Market

The first attack on Greenspan was one of those indirect, by-implication-only assaults in which government officials specialise. William Poole, president of the Federal Bank of St. Louis, used a speech to real estate (property) professionals to unburden himself of some thoughts on the non-prime mortgage market.

That market, Poole pointed out, matters to the Fed [Federal Reserve System] because of the importance of the housing industry to the overall economy, and the Fed's regulatory responsibility for banks and practices in the mortgage market. He therefore finds it "odd" that the Fed and lenders did not realise that low interest rates in the 2002–04 period could not be maintained. Yet sub-prime borrowers were encouraged to take out adjustable rate mortgages (ARMs), many of which are now in default as a result of higher interest rates, leaving a trail of foreclosures and chaos in the market for mortgage-backed securities. For most of these players Poole has little sympathy: "This year's markets punished mostly bad actors and/or poor lending practices. . . . The market's punishment of unsound financial arrangements has been swift, harsh and without prejudice."

Poole emphasizes that we are now dealing with a nontrivial problem. About 25 percent of the over $10 trillion in outstanding mortgages do not qualify for "prime" rating. And of the 50 million mortgages outstanding in America, 7.5 million are the obligation of subprime borrowers. It is the "relatively unsophisticated borrowers" for whom the regulators should have sympathy; they were inadequately protected from fraudulent and deceptive practices of greedy mortgage brokers and lenders.

Greenspan's main point was that, "American consumers might benefit if lenders provided greater mortgage product alternatives to the traditional fixed-rate mortgage."

What does all of this have to do with Greenspan, who is nowhere mentioned in Poole's rather elegant analysis? Fast forward one week, to the *New York Times* and columnist Floyd Norris. Norris points out that in 2004—a time when Poole argues any knowledgeable observer knew that interest rates were due to rise, the then–Fed chairman told credit union executives, in Norris's version, that "recent research within the Federal Reserve suggests that many homeowners might have saved tens of thousands of dollars had they held adjustable rate mortgages rather than fixed rate mortgages during the past decades."

A Misinformed Attack

Unfortunately, Norris fails to include the final phrase in the sentence he cites, or even to indicate the omission with the traditional ellipses. Greenspan concluded his report of the Fed's research with the comment, "though this would not have been the case, of course, had interest rates trended sharply upward." In short, Greenspan, who critics accuse of hostility to fixed rate mortgages, did indeed relate the savings from the use of ARMs to the low interest rates prevailing at the time of the Fed studies and his talk.

Greenspan's main point was that, "American consumers might benefit if lenders provided greater mortgage product alternatives to the traditional fixed-rate mortgage." That has certainly been the case, as Poole points out, ". . . The bottom line is that more people have access to mortgage credit now that ever before. . . . Despite its limitations and flaws, the non-prime market has served a large number of borrowers very well."

In short, the situation is roughly this: Mortgage brokers, who earn their income from commissions for initiating mortgages, made homeownership possible for many families for whom this American dream would otherwise have been denied. Some of these brokers failed to advise their unsophisticated customers of the dangers inherent in ARMs. Bankers then compounded the problem by bundling these relatively high-risk debts into packages that, they thought, magically turned a basket consisting of separate bits of high-risk paper into one package of low-risk paper. Which would have been the case had not all of the components been subject to the same risk—an increase in interest rates.

Now the market is giving the over-optimistic lenders their comeuppance, while institutions such as Freddie Mac [Federal Home Loan Mortgage Corporation] (a client), Fannie Mae [Federal National Mortgage Association], and other government agencies search for ways to relieve the plight of those among the over-extended homeowners who did not engage in fraud in order to obtain mortgages.

Will the New Chairman Get the Job Done?

Meanwhile, analysts are coping with the broader question of measuring the skill of various Federal Reserve Board chairmen in managing monetary policy—not merely as an historical exercise, but for clues to how competent the incumbent, Ben Bernanke, is likely to be in seeing America through the current period of volatile share prices, an ailing housing industry, and the turmoil in the financial sector as investors price risk more realistically.

Ray Fair, a fellow at the International Center for Finance at Yale University, in a paper that carries academic impenetrability to new heights, has compared the performance of the past five Federal Reserve chairmen. In perhaps the only clear statement in a jargon-laden, highly technical paper, Fair concludes, "Greenspan looks good . . ." in comparison with his four predecessors. Which should come as no surprise to those of us who watched him pilot the economy through the collapse of Long-Term Capital, the ruble, Asian developing economies, and a recession.

Fortunately, Bernanke, after an early loose-lipped stumble at a dinner party with CNBC's "Money Honey," Maria Bartiromo, and a bit of problem communicating his intentions to the markets (Bernankean clarity does not always trump Greenspanian opacity), has been demonstrating a similar deft touch. With "fear . . . sweeping through the financial markets," as Goldman Sachs puts it in its latest advisory, he faces a new, tougher test.

8

Racial Discrimination May Be an Issue in the Subprime Crisis

Algernon Austin

Algernon Austin is a sociologist of racial relations. He is the director of the Race, Ethnicity, and Economy program at the Economic Policy Institute.

Whites tend to blame the crisis on irresponsible behavior on the part of home buyers, who borrowed more than they could afford. Blacks however, are sensitive to claims that a disproportionate negative impact of the crisis has fallen on people of color, who were more likely to receive questionable loans. It is important to find out if discriminatory lending practices have been a contributing factor in the subprime mortgage crisis.

How the country responds or does not respond to the housing crisis could add to the long list of racial grievances. As Senator Barack Obama so effectively argued, race can play a big part in our perception of the world. My sense is that, to a degree, whites and blacks have very different readings of what happened to produce the housing crisis.

Of course, there is a diversity of views among whites and blacks, but in talking with people and reading articles, op-eds and reports, I've noticed certain tendencies. My evidence is anecdotal, so I could be wrong, but I would wager that in this issue, as in so many others, race matters.

Blacks and Whites See Things Differently

The whites I've encountered have tended to be more sympathetic to the tough-love approach espoused by Senator John McCain. They have talked about people who irresponsibly sought to purchase more house than they could afford. Or people who thought their home values would rise forever and used their homes like a machine that printed money. In these narratives, people who are facing foreclosure do not deserve much sympathy. They made their bed and they should lie in it.

The blacks that I've heard from bring a very different perspective to the issue. They think of the history of racial discrimination by the Federal Housing Authority. They also think of the recent findings of racial discrimination in lending from paired-tester studies. When these blacks hear of the disproportionate negative impact of the subprime crisis on people of color, their first suspicion is that once again racial discrimination was at play.

Were borrowers facing foreclosure greedy and irresponsible, or were they exploited by racially-biased predatory lenders looking to bundle and sell loans?

It is very difficult to determine to what extent either of these positions is true. But it is very important that we do find out. If we were to bail out large numbers of greedy and irresponsible borrowers, that would be bad. On the other hand, if we were to ignore the plight of large numbers of blacks who were taken advantage of by lenders, that would also be bad.

It is good to be aware that people have different perspectives on issues. These perspectives should be heard and understood. But, as difficult a time as the country has had in just acknowledging different perspectives, that acknowledgement is still the easy part of the problem.

We Need to Know if Minorities Were Exploited

The hard part is determining which perspective is right and getting everyone, or at least a majority of both sides, to agree on what the right answer is. Only when there is agreement on the right answer can a policy response be crafted that is seen as fair and appropriate by all and racial conflict avoided.

In the housing meltdown, it is quite possible that both positions are correct. It is possible that some people greedily pursued houses they could not afford. It is also possible that minority borrowers were exploited by lenders.

If we are going to bail out institutions involved in the crisis, the federal government should require that we learn exactly what went wrong. If lenders open their records to researchers at the Federal Reserve or the General Accounting Office, we can learn more about the people who borrowed and the homes they acquired. Were the homes extravagant or were the interest terms exorbitant and the deals shady?

It is clear that blacks were more likely to have subprime mortgages, but as lenders are quick to point out, this fact does not prove discrimination. Blacks tend to have more debt, lower incomes and much less wealth than whites, so it could be that blacks' generally worse credit scores placed them disproportionately in the subprime market. If the federal government commissioned a study with individual credit score data—used confidentially, of course—we could obtain very strong evidence on whether it was race or credit scores that placed so many blacks in the subprime market.

Armed with the findings of this research and with sensitivities to the long history of racial discrimination by financial institutions, the country could then move toward a sensible path to prevent us from ending up in this place again.

Recognizing that blacks and whites may come at issues like the housing crisis from different perspectives is an important insight. These perspectives need to be acknowledged and respected. But we can't end there. We need to figure out how we can get blacks and whites—and everybody else—to agree on a common vision of how we should move forward. That is the hard part.

9

Many Working Americans Cannot Afford a Home

Michael Grunwald

Michael Grunwald is a staff writer for the Washington Post.

Affordable housing supports community growth and enhances the quality of life, yet many working people in America today cannot afford to buy a home. This is a serious problem that deserves the attention of the political establishment, yet no one is talking about it.

In the past five years, housing prices in Fairfax County [Virginia] have grown 12 times as fast as household incomes. Today, the county's median family would have to spend 54 percent of its income to afford the county's median home; in 2000, the figure was 26 percent. The situation is so dire that Fairfax recently began offering housing subsidies to families earning $90,000 a year; soon, that figure may go as high as $110,000 a year.

Seventy years after President Franklin D. Roosevelt declared that the Depression had left one-third of the American people "ill-housed, ill-clothed and ill-nourished," Americans are well-clothed and increasingly overnourished. But the scarcity of affordable housing is a deepening national crisis, and not just for inner-city families on welfare. The problem has climbed the income ladder and moved to the suburbs, where service workers cram their families into overcrowded apartments, college graduates have to crash with their parents, and firefighters, police officers and teachers can't afford to live in the communities they serve.

The current crunch falls hardest on renters in Democratic-leaning cities and metropolitan areas, but Democrats have ignored the issue as resolutely as Republicans.

The Problem Is Becoming More Serious

Homeownership is near an all-time high, but the gap is growing between the Owns and the Own-Nots—as well as the Owns and the Own-80-Miles-From-Works. One-third of Americans now spend at least 30 percent of their income on housing, the federal definition of an "unaffordable" burden, and half the working poor spend at least 50 percent of their income on rent, a "critical" burden. The real estate boom of the past decade has produced windfalls for Americans who owned before it began, but affordable housing is now a [more] serious problem for more low- and moderate-income Americans than taxes, Social Security or gas prices.

Yet nobody in national politics is doing anything about it—or even talking about it.

For most of the past 70 years, housing was a bipartisan issue. In recent decades, its association with urban poverty made it more of a Democratic issue. But now it is simply a nonissue. The current crunch falls hardest on renters in Democratic-leaning cities and metropolitan areas, but Democrats have ignored the issue as resolutely as Republicans. Neither Sen. John F. Kerry (D-Mass.) nor President [George W.] Bush even bothered to propose affordable housing plans during the 2004 presidential campaign.

"Even 10 years ago, that would have been unimaginable," says Ron Utt of the conservative Heritage Foundation. "But now the problems are so much worse, and nobody cares. . . . I find myself on panels where I'm the token conservative, and I'm the one asking: Doesn't anyone care about affordable housing?"

America used to care a lot about affordable housing. Roosevelt signed housing legislation in 1934 and 1937, providing mortgages, government apartments and construction jobs for workers down on their luck. In 1949, Congress set an official goal of "a decent home and a suitable living environment for every American family," and in 1974, President Richard M. Nixon began offering subsidized rent vouchers to millions of low-income tenants in private housing. For half a century, most housing debates in Washington revolved around how much to expand federal assistance.

Today, Housing Is Not a Political Priority

But for the past two decades, the public face of public housing has been decrepit projects such as Chicago's Robert Taylor Homes and Cabrini-Green. And the only new federal housing initiative has been HOPE VI, a Clinton administration program that has demolished 80,000 units of the worst public housing and built mixed-income developments in their place. The program has eliminated most of the high-rise hellholes that gave public housing a bad name, including Robert Taylor and Cabrini-Green, and has revived some urban neighborhoods. But it has razed more subsidized apartments than it has replaced.

Overall, the number of households receiving federal aid has flatlined since the early 1990s, despite an expanding population and a ballooning budget. Congress has rejected most of President Bush's proposed cuts, but there has been virtually no discussion of increases; affordable-housing advocates spend most of their time fighting to preserve the status quo.

And it's a tough status quo. Today, for every one of the 4.5 million low-income families that receive federal housing assistance, there are three eligible families without it. Fairfax County has 12,000 families on a waiting list for 4,000 assisted apartments. "It's golden when you get one—nobody wants to give it up," says Conrad Egan, chairman of the Fairfax housing authority. It sounds odd, but the victims of today's housing crisis are not people living in "the projects," but people who aren't even that lucky.

Some liberals dream of extending subsidies to all eligible low-income families, but that $100 billion-a-year solution was unrealistic even before the budget deficit ballooned again. So even some housing advocates now support time limits on most federal rent aid. The time limits included in welfare reform 10 years ago were controversial, but studies suggest they've helped motivate recipients to get off the dole. And unlike welfare, housing aid is not a federal entitlement, so taking it away from one family after a few years would provide a break for an equally deserving family.

"It's a no-brainer," says David Smith, an affordable-housing advocate in Boston. "You can't sustain the internal contradiction of no limits."

Affordable housing . . . helps make communities competitive; it's not clear how Fairfax can keep creating jobs if workers can't afford to live there.

Smith and many local housing officials also think that the strict income limits for most federal housing aid serve as employment disincentives, while concentrating poor children in projects without working role models. Rents are usually set at 30 percent of income, so the lowest-income families pay virtually nothing, and as Smith points out, "it's economic suicide for them to get a job." But the vast gap between the number of low-income families eligible for subsidies and the number served suggests that tinkering with the current system would not come close to solving the crisis. And the problems extend well beyond low-income families, which is why communities such as Fairfax now assist middle-class renters.

The Demand Exceeds the Supply

The root of the problem is the striking mismatch between the demand for and the supply of affordable housing—or, more accurately, affordable housing near jobs. Fifteen million families now spend at least half their income on housing, according to Harvard's Joint Center for Housing Studies; many skimp on health care, child care and food to do so. Others reduce their rents by overcrowding, which studies link to higher crime rates, poorer academic performance and poorer health; Los Angeles alone has 620,000 homes with more than one person per room.

Other workers are enduring increasingly long commutes from less expensive communities, a phenomenon known as "driving to qualify." [From 2002–2007], 88,000 Fairfax County families have moved elsewhere in the region, according to a George Mason University study; when Fairfax housing officials gave me a tour recently, they told me many of their employees now drive a full hour from Warrenton in Fauquier County. The media officer interjected that she drives nearly two hours each way from Winchester in Frederick County. The driver said he lives in Winchester, too.

This creates all kinds of lousy outcomes—children who don't get to see their parents, workers who can't make ends meet when gas prices soar, exurban sprawl, roads clogged with long-distance commuters emitting greenhouse gases. "I don't think we're creating strong communities by forcing people into their cars four hours a day," says Cathy Hudgins, chairwoman of the housing committee for the Fairfax County Board of Supervisors. Affordable housing also helps make communities competitive; it's not clear how Fairfax can keep creating jobs if workers can't afford to live there.

Moderate-income families aren't able to buy Lamborghinis or Armani, but they can buy cars and clothes. So while it's obvious why they can't afford McMansions, it's not so obvious why they can't afford decent housing. They demand it. Shouldn't the market supply it?

The answer is yes. But in many communities, local regulations have stifled multifamily housing and even modest single-family housing. Minimum lot requirements, minimum parking requirements, density restrictions and other controls go well beyond the traditional mission of the building code and end up artificially reducing the development of safe, affordable housing.

Resistance to Widely Accessible Housing

The unfashionable but accurate term for these restrictions is "snob zoning." Suburbanites use them to boost property values by keeping out riffraff—even the riffraff who teach their kids, police their streets and extinguish their fires. Urbanites are susceptible to the same NIMBY [not in my backyard] impulses, often couched as opposition to "traffic congestion" or "overdevelopment" or protection of the neighborhood's "character." It's easy to support affordable housing in someone else's neighborhood. But when developers propose high-density projects, neighborhoods object.

Fairfax recently bucked that trend when it approved a developer's proposal to tear down 65 single-family houses across the street from the Vienna Metro station and replace them with 2,248 high-rise apartments. The project will increase the supply of job-accessible housing and take commuters out of their cars; the county is even forcing the developer to set aside a small percentage of moderate-income units in exchange for an exemption from its anti-density rules. But the Fairfax supervisors rejected a similar mega-project down the street, bowing to opponents worried about traffic congestion, property values and "the element" the high-rises might attract.

Still, Fairfax County illustrates how the creative solutions to the current crisis are emerging locally. It was one of 130 communities to adopt "inclusionary zoning," requiring developers to reserve a percentage of affordable units. It is one of more than 300 communities with affordable-housing trust funds; Fairfax voters approved a "Penny for Housing" initiative that will divert one cent of property taxes to subsidized projects. The Fairfax housing authority is also at the cutting edge of "workforce housing," offering 20 single-room apartments for day laborers in its own offices, while building and buying several dozen townhouses to rent to nurses, police officers, firefighters, teachers and bus drivers.

But these local projects address only a tiny fraction of the demand. For example, Los Angeles is considering a bond issue that would create 1,000 units of affordable housing—small comfort to those 620,000 families in overcrowded apartments. Economist Christopher Thornberg notes that California's private market added 120,000 urban rental units in 1987; in the first half of 2006, the total was just 232. The main obstacle, Thornberg concludes, is "the intransigence of local zoning boards."

In other words, the best thing local officials can do to promote affordable housing is to get out of the way—stop requiring one-acre lots and two-car garages, and stop blocking low-income and high-density projects.

The American Dream Is Far Out of Reach

Washington politicians, on the other hand, have the federal budget at their disposal. But Congress hasn't supported new construction since the Low-Income Housing Tax Credit of 1986, which creates nearly 100,000 units of affordable housing a year, enough to replace half the units that are torn down or converted to market rents. Bush proposed a home-ownership tax credit during his 2000 and 2004 campaigns, but it turned out to be the rare tax cut he didn't pursue. A bill pending in

Congress would divert a percentage of profits from federally chartered institutions such as Fannie Mae [Federal National Mortgage Association] to a national affordable-housing trust fund, but it seems stalled. The only affordability ideas with any traction at the national level are not really housing ideas; for example, one way to make housing more affordable to workers would be to raise their incomes—through higher minimum wages, lower payroll taxes or an expanded Earned Income Tax Credit.

There is one clear solution to the affordable-housing crisis: a real estate crash. It's the one housing issue that attracts media attentions—because it would hurt the Owns. But while an easing of prices could be devastating for lower-income Owns with risky mortgages, it probably wouldn't bring home ownership within reach for many Own-Nots. Prices have too far to fall; in 2000, two-thirds of the home sales in Fairfax were for $250,000 or less, but [in 2006], fewer than one-twentieth were. And even a modest price slump could trigger a construction slowdown that would make shortages of affordable housing for moderate-income families even worse.

Eventually, politicians may rediscover housing—not as an urban poverty issue, but as a middle-class quality-of-life issue, like gas prices or health care. Homeownership is often described as the American dream, but these days many workers would settle for a decent rental that won't bankrupt their families.

10

The Government Should Focus on Families That Have Lost Their Homes

Paul Weinstein Jr.

Paul Weinstein Jr. is the chief operating officer and a senior fellow at the Progressive Policy Institute. He lectures at Johns Hopkins University.

The ongoing housing slump is having a devastating effect on many American families, who now own properties that are worth less than their original purchase price, and who are finding it difficult to refinance adjustable-rate mortgages (ARMs). There are three things Congress can do to help families caught up in this crisis: They can expand the Homebuyers Tax Credit, establish a temporary emergency housing voucher program, and utilize the resources of government-sponsored enterprises to increase funds available to refinance mortgages on more sustainable terms.

A merica is in the midst of the worst housing slump in 16 years. Across the country, home sales are in decline, and prices are falling. In some states, the housing slump has been particularly severe. In Florida, sales in the second quarter of [2007] were down 41.3 percent compared to the same period [in 2006], while in Nevada they dropped by 37.5 percent. Many other states have had declines of 20 percent or more, including Arizona, Tennessee, and Maryland. Nationwide, the overall decline was nearly 11 percent from last year. As a re-

Paul Weinstein Jr., "Gimme Shelter: Three Ideas to Protect the American Dream of Homeownership," *Progressive Policy Institute*, October 2007. Reproduced by permission. http://www.ppionline.org/ppi_ci.cfm?kaid=125&subid=162&contentid=254479.

sult, many families are holding onto properties that are now worth less than their original purchase value.

Millions of homeowners are now trapped. . . . They can't afford to sell, because they paid more for their house than it is now worth; nor can they afford the new, higher mortgage rates.

$1 Trillion Worth of Loans Are in Jeopardy

While home sales are slumping, of equal concern is the rising number of Americans who are losing their homes because they are no longer able to make their monthly mortgage payments. In the second quarter of 2007, the percentage of U.S. mortgages entering the foreclosure process set a new record, according to a September report by the Mortgage Bankers Association. That record is sure to be broken many times in [2008] as more than $1 trillion dollars worth of adjustable-rate mortgages (ARMs) are due to reset between [October 2007] and November 2008.

Over the last decade, subprime lending has grown at an explosive pace, reaching nearly $1.2 trillion in mortgages outstanding. The practice has helped increase the share of families that own their homes to a record 69 percent, from about 65 percent a few years ago, with much of that increase among minorities. It has become clear, however, that some lending practices in the subprime market were questionable and that disclosure of the requirements of these loans—such as prepayment penalties and the real possibility of higher interest-rate payments at a later time—were not explained or even downplayed by some lenders.

Furthermore, toward the end of the housing boom, when interest rates reached some of their lowest levels, lenders became more aggressive about marketing their services to borderline applicants. In many cases, these applicants lacked the financial wherewithal to meet their mortgage payments if market conditions changed (such as a drop in home prices coinciding with the expiration of low, "teaser" interest rates). As a result, millions of homeowners are now trapped in a financial stranglehold: They can't sell, because they paid more for their house than it is now worth; nor can they afford the new, higher mortgage rates.

Too little attention has been paid to helping the millions of families who have lost or will lose their homes.

More Americans Will Lose Their Homes

As a result, the delinquency rate on subprime loans has soared recently to approximately 13 percent, and most analysts predict that it will climb much higher, especially as the teaser rates on some 2 million subprime mortgages must be reset by the end of 2008. (A reset is the point in time when the teaser rate on certain types of mortgages—like subprime products—expires and a new rate—usually much higher—becomes effective.) That means even more Americans will lose their homes, including a significant share of minority families who have only recently been able to claim their piece of the American Dream. Furthermore, the loss of individual homes could spiral into a broader problem for many communities, as neighborhoods beset by foreclosure signs become vulnerable to blight and a loss of economic vitality.

In Congress, many leaders on both sides of the aisle have offered proposals to prevent some of the most abusive and predatory lending practices. These ideas include legislation to prohibit mortgage brokers from steering people into subprime loans if they qualify for cheaper conventional mortgages; a ban on hidden brokerage fees that are rolled into higher interest rates; and a halt on prepayment penalties that make it difficult for people to refinance.

Congress Should Focus on Families

While these may be worthy prescriptions, there remains a more basic problem. Too little attention has been paid to helping the millions of families who have lost or will lose their homes. In this policy brief, the Progressive Policy Institute offers three proposals to help those families who have already lost their homes—and reduce the number of those who are at risk of future foreclosure:

- Expand the First-Time Homebuyers Tax Credit (HBTC) beyond the District of Columbia and allow those who have been victims of foreclosure to use the credit to purchase new homes;

- Establish a temporary emergency housing voucher program to help those who are struggling to make payments on their subprime mortgages stay in their homes; and

- Utilize Fannie Mae [Federal National Mortgage Association] and Freddie Mac [Federal Home Loan Mortgage Corporation] to provide temporary liquidity and stability to the housing market.

Expand the Homebuyers Tax Credit

One the most successful community development initiatives of the 1990s was the HBTC for Washington, D.C. Put into place by the [Bill] Clinton administration and Congress in 1997, the HBTC has been, according to a study published by the Fannie Mae Foundation in March 2005, "an effective policy instrument for increasing the first-time homeownership rate."

Like many cities, Washington D.C., has struggled to create an environment that would attract and retain middle-income families. In 1997, more than 10,000 people moved out of the nation's capital, bringing the net loss of population during the first seven years of the 1990s to 78,000. One way to entice people to return to the inner city was to provide more affordable housing opportunities. It was this rationale that led to the enactment of the HBTC in the nation's capital.

According to the Fannie Mae Foundation study, among program participants, first-time homebuyers represented 67 percent of all District homeowners between 1997 and 2005, significantly outpacing the national first-time homebuyer average (40 percent) and the central-city average (51 percent) for the same period. Furthermore, while the majority of credit claimants were already living in the District, some 14 percent were from the nearby suburbs, a number that was rising over time. Finally, and maybe most importantly, lower-income buyers (which, in the relatively expensive D.C. market, meant those with incomes between $30,000 and $50,000), formed the largest group of those taking advantage of the HBTC.

The HBTC is fairly straightforward. The credit is available to first-time District homebuyers. The legislation defines a first-time buyer as someone who has had "no present ownership interest in a principal residence in the District during the one-year period ending on the date of purchase." . . .

The one-year test differs from some other first-time buyer benefits available nationally. The credit is not limited to current city residents. Someone who owns a home in the suburbs is eligible so long as they meet the other criteria. A buyer who previously owned a D.C. home but has been renting a principal residence for more than a year also would be eligible. An otherwise ineligible homeowner cannot marry his or her way into the credit—both spouses must be individually eligible in order for a couple to take advantage of this benefit. The HBTC is for one-time use only. Unlike some other tax incentives, it applies to buyers in any D.C. neighborhood—not just economically distressed areas.

The HBTC Could Help Eligible Buyers Recover

The amount of the HBTC varies according to the buyer's income. A single taxpayer with modified adjusted gross income of less than $70,000 is eligible for the entire $5,000 tax credit. The credit phases out between $70,000 and $90,000 in modified adjusted gross income.

Joint filers are eligible for the entire credit as long as their modified adjusted gross income is less than $110,000; the benefit phases out between $110,000 and $130,000. Unmarried taxpayers who purchase a residence jointly will be allowed to split the credit. Unused portions of the credit can be carried over to future tax years.

As the experience in Washington, D.C., has proven, the HBTC could be an effective tool in helping families and neighborhoods recover from the damage created by the subprime market collapse. Expanding the HBTC to other cities could potentially increase the first-time homebuyer average by up to 16 percent, potentially reducing the foreclosure rate in hard-hit communities.

Under this proposal, the HBTC would be expanded to 10 high-risk communities—places where the subprime market collapse has been particularly severe. Communities that have high foreclosure rates could apply for HBTC designation for up to five years. Communities would be judged on their plans to match the HBTC with tax incentives or other housing programs of their own. To provide them a second chance, those families who lost homes due to the subprime market collapse and who held one of the dominant subprime mortgages (228 or 327 ARM products) would, along with first-time homebuyers, also be allowed to take the HBTC. (The program would apply to primary residences only.)

Expanding the HBTC to 10 cities would cost an estimated $450 million [through 2012]. If policymakers wanted to expand the program further, they could reduce the HBTC to $2,500 and double the number of communities to 20.

Establish a Housing Voucher Program

Created in the 1970s, the Section 8 housing voucher program has become the dominant form of federal housing assistance.

Low-income families use vouchers to help pay for housing that they find in the private market. The program is federally funded, but vouchers are distributed by a network of 2,400 local, state, and regional housing agencies. A family with a voucher is generally required to contribute 30 percent of its income for rent and utilities. The voucher then pays the rest of those costs, up to a limit (called a "payment standard") set by the housing agency.

The demand for housing vouchers is roughly three times greater than the supply.

Income-eligibility limits for the voucher program are set as percentages of the median income in the local area. Each year, the U.S. Department of Housing and Urban Development (HUD) estimates the median income for households of different sizes in every metropolitan area and rural county in the nation. State and local housing agencies have substantial flexibility to determine which families they will serve and are permitted to establish admission preferences based on household characteristics (such as preferences for working families, families that live in particular areas, or the currently homeless).

While vouchers are primarily used by families to help meet their rental payments, they can also be deployed to help with mortgage payments, enabling low-income families to purchase homes. In addition, up to 20 percent of voucher funds can be used for subsidies—called "project-based" vouchers—that are tied to a building rather than to a particular family, and which can help pay for the construction or rehabilitation of housing for low-income families. The cost of the current Section 8 voucher program is $15.9 billion annually, funding just over 2 million vouchers nationwide.

Unfortunately, the demand for housing vouchers is roughly three times greater than the supply. Therefore, policymakers should create a temporary category of 100,000 new vouchers under a special program that would sunset after three years. These vouchers would target families who have purchased 228 and 327 subprime loans and are at risk of losing their home (primary residences only) or have already suffered foreclosure (primary residences only).

Recipients could use the vouchers to help make their mortgage payments while they work with their lenders on identifying new mortgage products that might have a higher payment than their teaser rate, but a lower one than their reset rate. In addition, if they lose their homes, families could use the vouchers to help defray rent payments. As these families get back on their feet, the dollar amount of the voucher could be reduced. In total, families would only be qualified to receive these vouchers for up to 12 months, after which the vouchers would be made available to other eligible families. The total cost for this program would be $768 million each year.

Tap the Resources of Fannie Mae and Freddie Mac

There has been much debate in recent years over the regulation of Fannie Mae and Freddie Mac in the wake of accounting irregularities at both of these government-sponsored enterprises (GSEs). As result, both GSEs have agreed to place caps on their portfolios. Despite past problems, it makes little sense to ignore the tremendous potential of these organizations to provide much-needed liquidity and stability to the housing marketplace.

Sen. Charles Schumer (D [Democrat]-N.Y.) has introduced legislation entitled the "Protecting Access to Safe Mortgages Act." This law would temporarily lift the limits on GSEs' mortgage portfolios by 10 percent, which would free up approximately $145 billion for the purchase of new mortgages. An approach like this—with a "flexible goal" of 25 percent to 50 percent of the total going specifically toward refinanced mortgages for borrowers whose existing adjustable-rate loans were scheduled for an interest rate reset between June 2005 and December 2009—is a sensible compromise that will allow the GSEs to help restore confidence.

While this policy would give current and aspiring home-buyers greater confidence in the security and stability of the mortgage market, it would also help fund foreclosure-relief efforts across the country before the "October surprise" of subprime resets further shocks the mortgage markets. One trillion dollars worth of ARMs are due to reset between [October 2007] and November of 2008. Fannie Mae has estimated that 1.5 million subprime homeowners who face resetting ARMs and potential payment shocks [in 2007 and 2008] would qualify for a safe, fixed-rate loan backed by the GSEs. The Bush administration, instead of playing politics with the economic security of millions of Americans, should let the GSEs help restore stabilily and confidence to the housing marketplace.

Home ownership represents both an individual good and a community interest.

Home Ownership Is in the National Interest

The housing sector has been a powerful catalyst of the national economy, as millions of Americans have bought homes for the first time—and millions more have watched their largest investment appreciate in value.

Even these vast contributions to American prosperity do not capture the full economic and social importance of a healthy housing market—as people became more willing to invest in the purchase and upkeep of their houses, once-neglected neighborhoods revived; the construction and home-improvement industries prospered; and, most importantly, home-owning individuals and families made vital investments in their own future and the future of their communities.

Underlying all of these beneficial developments was a sense of security—namely, the security of one's own status as a homeowner and the security of the housing market as a whole. It is precisely this sense of security that has been undermined in the subprime housing crisis.

This is a solvable problem, however, and the solution lies in recognizing the need for stronger institutional protections for homeowners, particularly the more vulnerable buyers who have purchased homes on the subprime market. Some of the potential solutions are temporary, such as the emergency-voucher program outlined above. Other useful fixes would be of a more lasting nature, including the expansion of the highly promising HBTC.

What these solutions have in common is a recognition that home ownership represents both an individual good and a community interest. Indeed, this is the understanding that lies at the root of the mortgage-interest deduction in our tax code. It is in our national interest to encourage home ownership, and to offer carefully targeted assistance to ensure that this hallmark of the American Dream remains attainable, and sustainable, for as many Americans as possible.

11

The Government Should Print More Money to Free Up Funds for Lending

John H. Makin

John H. Makin is a visiting scholar at the American Enterprise Institute.

Recently, average home prices have fallen at a 23 percent annual rate, and they will almost certainly fall another 25 to 30 percent, unless action is taken to free up money for mortgages. The best alternative, though not one without risk, is for the Federal Reserve to stabilize housing prices by printing money.

The policy alternatives in the post-housing-bubble world are painfully unpleasant. In my view, the least bad option is for the Federal Reserve [Fed] to print money to help stabilize housing prices and financial markets. Yes, use reflation to soften the pain for Main Street and Wall Street. If instead we let housing prices fall another 25%–30%—as predicted by the Case-Shiller Home Price Index—it's almost certain that Washington will end up nationalizing the mortgage business.

So far, the Fed's lending programs have not provided adequate liquidity to financial markets: Reserves supplied to the banking system have grown at a tiny 0.6% annual rate since December [2007]. That's because the reserves the Fed is injecting by lending are effectively pulled out or "sterilized" by its sales of Treasury securities. The Fed has been selling these securities to keep the fed funds rate at the level targeted by its Federal Open Market Committee directives.

Borrowers Cannot Get Credit

Congress and the Treasury have proposed voluntary measures to help mortgage borrowers, but the impact on mortgage availability has been nil. As average house prices plummet—declining at a 23% annual rate over the three months ending in January [2008]—lenders are sharply curtailing access to mortgage-based, home-equity loans. The 15% of U.S. mortgage holders with negative equity in their homes have no access to credit, and 20% with marginal equity have limited access at best. Overall access to credit is contracting: Ask Americans trying to utilize home-equity lines or arrange student loans.

The monetary easing I'm recommending can occur by having the Fed print money to purchase mortgages directly, or purchase Treasury securities directly.

Meanwhile, the collapse of house prices and the attendant damage to credit markets have become so severe that the Fed has been forced to create new policy measures at a fast clip, including the radical decision to take $30 billion worth of Bear Stearns' risky mortgages onto its own balance sheet, and to open the discount window to investment banks.

The bottom line is this: The Fed could have watched a run on investment banks quickly turn into a run on commercial banks, or protected the creditors of investment banks (like the depositors of commercial banks) at the expense of Bear Stearns' shareholders. The Fed wisely chose the second alternative.

Still, the Fed's intervention has done no more than buy a respite from the crisis in the financial markets. The monetary easing I'm recommending can occur by having the Fed print money to purchase mortgages directly, or purchase Treasury securities directly. The latter is probably more desirable because it adds higher-quality assets to the Fed's balance sheet. The Bank of Japan was also forced to reflate by printing money in 2001, after two years of a zero interest-rate policy failed to lift the economy out of a prolonged recession that had moved Japan to the brink of a deflationary crisis.

Risking a Recession

Fed reflation—to slow the fall in home prices and alleviate the distress for households and lenders—carries many risks. But the alternative is to struggle with a patchwork of inadequate efforts to shore up mortgage markets, while the Fed sticks to its current tactic of pegging the fed funds rate without increasing the money supply. This, I would submit, is even more risky. It risks a severe recession that will only intensify the drive for reregulation of financial and mortgage markets after the election.

> *Injection of money holds some promise of alleviating the worst of the credit crisis. This means that, after the [2008] election, Congress will not feel justified in nationalizing mortgage markets.*

Printing money is a radical step that enables the Fed to stop pegging the federal-funds rate and start increasing market liquidity directly. In any event, there is substantial evidence that the fed funds rate has been well above the equilibrium level. One piece of evidence is the accelerating deterioration in credit markets and the real economy that ensued even while the Fed cut the rate. Even more compelling, consider the sharp widening of the gap between the fed funds rate and the yield on three-month Treasury bills.

That gap, usually close to zero, measures the intensity of demand for riskless assets relative to the Fed's target rate in the interbank market. At the time of the Bear Stearns crisis [when an emergency loan from the Fed failed to prevent collapse, the bank was sold] the fed funds rate was an extraordinary 250 basis points above yields on three-month Treasurys. This corresponded to a "10 sigma," or ten-times-the-typical deviation from the mean event. Statistically, 2 or 3 sigma is a very unusual event suggesting, in this case, an unusually strong preference for riskless T-bills [Treasury bills]. Four or 5 sigma represents a serious risky event, and 10 sigma is an outright panic. Based on this gap criterion, the August 2007 crisis onset was a 5-sigma event, while the October 1998 LTCM [Long-Term Capital Management hedge fund] crisis and the 1987 stock market crash were each 4-sigma events. This suggests that even at those earlier times of crisis there was less fear as expressed by a run into riskless Treasurys. Ominously, after dipping close to 5 sigma after the Bear Stearns crisis, the gap has crept back above 6 sigma.

The Fed should announce its intention to add to its holding of Treasury securities in order to provide additional liquidity. It should cease pegging the fed funds rate while this policy is in effect. While there is no guarantee, direct injection of money holds some promise of alleviating the worst of the credit crisis. This means that, after the [2008] election, Congress will not feel justified in nationalizing mortgage markets.

While there is a substantial risk that inflation may rise for a time—this would be the policy goal—monetization is more easily reversible than nationalization of the mortgage market. Meanwhile, Fed officials concerned about inflation should rethink their view that it is impossible to identify an asset bubble before it bursts.

The postbubble period has yielded some very unattractive policy alternatives. They clearly underscore the rationale for having the Fed target asset prices—in a world where asset markets affect the real economy more than the real economy affects asset markets.

12

The Lending Industry Should Be Regulated to Protect Consumers

Neal Peirce

Neal Peirce is a founder of the National Journal *and former political editor of* Congressional Quarterly. *He is the author of 12 books, including* Citistates: How Urban America Can Prosper in a Competitive World.

Washington bears a lot of blame for the housing slump and subprime lending crisis. It gave in to pressure from Wall Street and the financial services industry, and deregulated the U.S. housing finance market, opening the door to trillions of dollars in bad loans that have led to the collapse of housing prices. Washington needs to return to the strong regulatory environment of the past, including verification of income and licensing of stockbrokers and insurance brokers. Adjustable-rate mortgages (ARMs) should no longer be allowed.

Can it be as bad as some say—2 million home foreclosures in 2008, the worst housing slump since the Great Depression? Will there be heartbreak for so many more families, boarded-up windows and abandonment ravaging vulnerable neighborhoods coast to coast?

The prognosis is not favorable. Subprime lending—mortgages with interest rates that suddenly escalate after a few years, forcing often naive and unprepared homeowners to default—has taken a heavy toll. Houses vacated by foreclosures are deteriorating into eyesores, encouraging crime, depressing property values, costing localities revenues they need for schools, police and other vital services.

Is there a villain in this story? Yes, and he's hidden in plain view: a heavily lobbied federal government that lost sight of ordinary Americans' interests.

Some Northeastern cities—Cleveland, Buffalo, Pittsburgh among them—are said to be the hardest hit. Among the states, Florida, California and Indiana are registering the most foreclosures.

But the pain is being felt nationwide. The U.S. Conference of Mayors projects the weak housing market and large inventory of unsold homes may reduce cumulative U.S. home values by $1.2 trillion [in 2008].

Is there a villain in this story? Yes, and he's hidden in plain view: a heavily lobbied federal government that lost sight of ordinary Americans' interests.

Deregulation Has Hurt the Housing Finance Market

That's the story told in *The American Prospect* magazine by John Atlas of the National Housing Institute and Peter Dreier, a professor of politics at Occidental College in Los Angeles. The problem, they say, is that Washington succumbed to pressure from Wall Street and other financial players and deregulated a once stable, smoothly functioning American housing finance market. And that the only way out is a U-turn, back to circa 1970 or earlier in national regulation.

The history is illuminating. The ravages of the Depression triggered a range of bank regulations and agencies to protect consumers, among them the Federal Deposit Insurance Corporation [FDIC], the Federal Home Loan Bank System, Fannie Mae [Federal National Mortgage Association] and the Federal Housing Administration. The savings and loan industry was highly regulated, its mission to take people's deposits and use them exclusively for home mortgages.

Washington also insured loans through the FDIC, created a secondary market to keep capital flowing, and required S&Ls [savings and loan associations] to make predictable 30-year fixed-rate loans. Homeownership soared and there were few foreclosures.

But in the early 1980s the politically powerful lending industry convinced Congress to eliminate interest-rate caps and loosen mortgage controls. The S&Ls got permission to compete with conventional banks, then began a decade-long orgy of real estate speculation. Banks and S&Ls started devouring each other and making loans for shopping malls, golf courses and condo projects with scant financial logic. Result: By the late '80s, hundreds of banks and S&Ls went under and the federal government had to step in to bail out depositors.

Simply forbid adjustable-rate mortgages because they're just as risky . . . as playing the stock market.

In the aftermath, with stable S&Ls vanished and federal controls emasculated, a giant "financial services" industry of banks, insurance companies, credit card firms and other money lenders emerged. Mortgage brokers, Atlas and Dreier charge, became "the street hustlers of the lending world," making a fee for each borrower they recruited and handed over to a mortgage lender—often collecting an extra fee in return for negotiating an inflated interest rate.

Large mortgage finance companies began to make massive profits on subprime loans. Wall Street in recent years created special investment units to buy up those mortgages from the lenders, bundling them into mortgage-backed securities and selling them (at fat fees) to unsuspecting investors around the world.

Dark Clouds over an Entire Industry

But when thousands of the unregulated mortgages started to go south, the present collapse was triggered, with billion-dollar losses for Wall Street firms and dark clouds across all mortgage lending.

So how should we recover? President [George W.] Bush's so-called interest-rate "freeze," announced in late fall [2007], is hardly the answer. It's entirely voluntary and is projected to apply to only 12 percent of the mortgage holders—none already in default in 2007—that are likely to have severe difficulty making their monthly payments.

Some better ideas are before Congress, including a recently House-passed bill that requires lenders to verify all applicants' income and document their credit-worthiness. Mortgage companies and brokers would have to be licensed, like stockbrokers and insurance brokers.

But Dreier tells me he'd go further—for example, simply forbid adjustable-rate mortagages because they're just as risky, he insists, as playing the stock market. And he'd strengthen nonprofit lenders such as the federally chartered Neighborhood Housing Services of America [NSHA]. NHSA has made thousands of loans to low-income borrowers with an enviable delinquency rate of just 3.34 percent—mostly because it requires every borrower to take its strong mortgage education program before and after a loan is made.

"Daylighting" the lending process, putting tight rules on all mortgage lending? Would those moves be too restrictive, harm our free market? No way, I'd say. Strong regulations led post–World War II America toward world-leading home-ownership rates and an expansive economy. Capitalism works best with clear rules. Let's go back there.

13

Smarter Buyers and Tougher Lending Standards Are Needed

Hans L. Schwendimann

Hans L. Schwendimann is a graduate research assistant at the Sparks Bureau of Business and Economic Research's Center for Real Estate Development.

Real estate professionals and homeowners are worried about the housing market and the mortgage lending market, as a result of record-high numbers of foreclosures in many markets across the country. Forecasts indicate home prices will continue to decline through 2009. While many factors worked together to create the crisis, and while no clear solution presents itself, there is a need for buyers to be smarter about taking on debt, and for lenders to be more thorough in screening potential buyers, in order to stabilize the housing market.

The startling foreclosure numbers revealed by RealtyTrac in January 2007 and the recent fallout in the subprime mortgage market have left real estate professionals and homeowners questioning the vitality of the housing market and the future of the residential mortgage market. Although many theories exist as to why foreclosure filings in the United States increased 42 percent in 2006, these theories have failed to identify the factors unique to various regions that contribute to the demise of specific markets.

If research already conducted on this matter has shown anything, it is that there is no single cause behind the growing

Hans L. Schwendimann, "The Mortgage Default Crisis: The American Dream Becomes a Nightmare," *Business Perspectives*, Summer 2007. Copyright © 2007 University of Memphis. Reproduced by permission of the author.

problem. The dramatic payment increases in adjustable-rate mortgages (ARMs) shoulder the majority of the blame, appearing to be the leading cause in many locations. However, unemployment and a slowing in home-value appreciation also have been identified as contributing factors in other areas. Supporting the preceding claim, the Mortgage Bankers Association reported in March 2007 that existing home prices deteriorated more than those of new homes over the last half of 2006. In addition to slowing appreciation, it was reported that the median price of existing homes on the market nationwide had declined in January [2007] for a sixth consecutive month.

Job Losses Contributed to the Problem

Several Midwestern states have felt the sting of foreclosure as a result of the substantial loss of manufacturing jobs due to cutbacks at General Motors, Ford, Chrysler, and several automotive parts suppliers. Unemployment rates in Michigan, Ohio, Illinois, and Indiana rose considerably over 2006, with some states reporting unemployment rates over 2 percent higher than the national average. The loss of jobs in the automotive industry contributed to Detroit's reporting the highest foreclosure rate of the nation's 100 largest metropolitan statistical areas in 2006 and resulted in Michigan having the fifth-highest foreclosure rate in the country.

It is possible that these Midwestern states never experienced a housing boom as did many regions and were consequently the first places to suffer the effects of declining home values. As in many other parts of the country, Midwestern homeowners ultimately found themselves with negative equity in their home as the value of their property fell below the remaining balance on their promissory note. Coupled with the rise in unemployment in the Midwest, borrowers in the region had few, if any, options to escape foreclosure.

Colorado and California are two states that did experience surges in their respective housing markets but are now struggling to maintain stability as a result of the increase in fore-closure filings. In 2006, Colorado reported the highest foreclo-sure rate in the country, and California generated the second-highest number of foreclosure filings. Analysts in both areas have indicated that the slowing housing market has resulted in one that requires additional time on the market for homes to sell. As a result, the supply of homes for sale in these states continues to rise.

Buyers Have Some Options

Depending on the circumstances, borrowers in default have the following options to avoid foreclosure:

- Bring their payments current,

- Refinance out of the default,

- Sell their home and pocket any net proceeds from the sale, or

- Convey a deed in lieu of foreclosure to their lender in some instances.

Those who have owned their home for a short time usu-ally opt to sell the property upon default. The slowing hous-ing market in many areas has left a significant number of these new homeowners with foreclosure as their final option. With little or no equity in their homes at the time of default, these homeowners are forced to sell their homes for the re-maining balance on the mortgage, if possible, and do not have the luxury of adjusting the selling price or keeping the home on the market for the time necessary for it to sell.

Adding to the problem in many of the formerly "boom-ing" markets is the likelihood of negative amortization in some option ARMs. When buyers purchase homes beyond their means in hopes of dramatic appreciation in value, many choose to make a fixed monthly payment early in the life of the loan that does not cover monthly interest charges. Left with a balance greater than the one at the time of origination, these borrowers have little chance to escape foreclosure with the slowing housing market and declining home values.

A Unique Situation

Memphis does not seem to parallel any of the other ailing areas in the country. Unlike most areas, Memphis has shown a consistent increase in home values over the last decade and actually experienced a significant decrease in the unemployment rate in 2006. Memphis, however, did rank second in the nation in February 2007 in the rate of subprime loans originated, accounting for 24 percent of all loan originations.

Just as Detroit and Denver represent the majority of foreclosure filings in Michigan and Colorado, Memphis consistently reports the majority of foreclosure filings in Tennessee. The 18,155 foreclosure filings reported in Memphis in 2006 represented over 49 percent of the total number of foreclosure filings reported in Tennessee for the year.

The high turnover rate of foreclosed properties in Hickory Hill and similar neighborhoods has given rise to the suspicion of predatory lending in the areas.

In Memphis, the foreclosure problem can even be broken down into specific neighborhoods, with Hickory Hill receiving much of the attention during this market turbulence. . . . This area is a prime example of a location that has reported a tremendous amount of foreclosure filings driven by local factors.

After it was annexed by the City of Memphis on December 31, 1998, Hickory Hill experienced a major demographic shift. After the annexation, the black population increased 450 percent, while the white population decreased 50 percent. In addition, Hickory Hill is now home to the city's largest Hispanic population after seeing an increase of 700 percent in Hispanic residents after the annexation. Unfortunately, over the last decade, Hickory Hill has transformed into a predominantly low-income area that has experienced dramatic increases in crime, bankruptcy filings, foreclosure filings, and slowing home-value appreciation.

The high turnover rate of foreclosed properties in Hickory Hill and similar neighborhoods has given rise to the suspicion of predatory lending in the areas. Although difficult to pinpoint with certainty, these Memphis neighborhoods inhabited by minorities, elderly, and low-income families are targets for abusive lending practices, especially when given the fact that Memphis has not seen the decrease in home values that other regions have.

The Long-Term Mortgage Finance Forecast issued by the Mortgage Bankers Association of America indicates that the housing market will continue to decline through 2007 and beyond. It is projected that housing starts, mortgage originations, and overall home sales will decline through 2009. Home-building activity is expected to decrease 18 percent in 2007 and is not projected to return to 2006 levels through 2009. Compared to 2005 levels, refinance originations are expected to decrease by over 40 percent by 2009 as 30-year fixed interest rates are expected to increase by 40 basis points.

The Lending Environment Is Risky

The condition of the housing market has created a very risky environment for both lenders and borrowers. Ideally, lenders would auction a foreclosed property as soon as possible to satisfy the remaining balance on the loan. However, today's slowing market and declining property values have left many lenders with substantial liability for homes they have been unable to sell. Adding to the risk in liquidating a lender's "other real estate owned" are the individual foreclosure laws observed in each state.

It can be argued that the lending environment is less risky in Tennessee and in other states that are dominated by the deed of trust custom. By conveying to a third party the power to sell a property upon the borrower's default, the costly and very lengthy judicial foreclosure process is eliminated. Additionally, deed of trust states typically require the borrower to waive the statutory right of redemption, which is the borrower's right to satisfy a default after a successful foreclosure sale, a practice that can dramatically extend the liquidation period and increases the liability to the lender.

Following the deed of trust custom results in a greater amount of foreclosures as evidenced by data provided by RealtyTrac. Lenders operating in deed of trust states potentially have a greater number of properties to liquidate, and the success of this process is determined by conditions in the housing and residential mortgage markets. The current condition of the market increases the liquidity risk to the lender and increases the possibility of the lender being forced to obtain a deficiency judgment against the borrower if the proceeds from the foreclosure sale are insufficient to satisfy the remaining balance on the loan.

Only an increase in borrower awareness and tougher lending standards will force potential homebuyers to realize the impossibility of continually making mortgage payments that are clearly beyond their means.

The Future Looks Grim

The data released for the first quarter of 2007 do not suggest a road to recovery. Foreclosure filings in Memphis increased over 15 percent from the fourth quarter of 2006, which is typically the worst quarter for filings. Even more disturbing is the fact that there were 1,738 more foreclosure filings in Memphis than there were home sales in the first quarter of [2007], generating a ratio of one home sale for every 1.46 foreclosure filings. Overall, foreclosure filings increased 27 percent from the fourth quarter of 2006 and resulted in a 35 percent year-over-year increase.

The various factors affecting individual markets already are taking their toll on struggling homeowners in 2007, and this growing problem shows no immediate signs of slowing. It will likely take years for the housing and residential mortgage markets to be extricated from this problem as troublesome adjustable rate mortgages continue to reset and push borrowers closer to default. These problem loans should continue to lose popularity, and borrowers will resign themselves to traditional fixed-rate mortgages in the near future.

As evidenced by the overwhelming increase in foreclosure filings, the American dream can quickly turn into a nightmare. Only an increase in borrower awareness and tougher lending standards will force potential homebuyers to realize the impossibility of continually making mortgage payments that are clearly beyond their means.

14

The Government Should Not Bail Out Problem Mortgages

David C. John

David C. John is senior research fellow in retirement security and financial institutions in the Thomas A. Roe Institute for Economic Policy Studies at the Heritage Foundation.

H.R. 5830 is a bill to provide support for existing at-risk mortgages by refinancing them through the Federal Housing Administration. Those refinanced loans would be guaranteed by the federal government. Congress is under great pressure to do something about the large number of mortgages that are likely to default. However, this is not a good solution to the problem. A preferable solution would be a voluntary private-sector plan that would not leave taxpayers responsible in the event that home buyers default on their newly refinanced loans.

Chairman Barney Frank (D [Democrat]-MA) of the House Financial Services Committee has proposed H.R. 5830, which would use the Federal Housing Administration (FHA) to refinance at-risk mortgages at a lower interest rate in return for a cash fee. Under the legislation, lenders that chose to take part in the voluntary program would agree to receive 85 percent of the current assessed value of the house, while the borrower would receive a refinanced loan equal to 90 percent of that new assessed value. Refinanced loans would be 100 percent guaranteed by the FHA, and the new lender would have

David C. John, "H.R. 5830, the Frank-Dodd FHA Refinance Plan, Is Still the Wrong Policy," *Heritage Foundation WebMemo* 1918, May 6, 2008. Copyright © 2008 The Heritage Foundation. Reproduced by permission. http://www.heritage.org/research/economy/wm1918.cfm.

no further credit exposure if the borrower subsequently defaulted. If the homeowner subsequently walked away from the new loan, and if the FHA lacked the resources to back the loan, then the taxpayers would cover any losses.

H.R. 5830 is a revised version of an earlier proposal by both Chairman Frank and Chairman Christopher Dodd (D-CT) of the Senate Banking Committee. While it is an improvement in some ways over the original plan, it still has many problems that make it the wrong way to deal with housing finance problems.

The Congressional Budget Office estimates that fully one-third of refinanced mortgages under H.R. 5830 will subsequently default.

A Wrong-Headed Plan

The proposal has many shortcomings. Specifically:

It is essentially a government buyout of problem mortgages disguised as a refinancing plan.

It is an extremely bad precedent, as lenders will quickly request that this guarantee be made available for all loans to borrowers with poor credit histories or lower incomes. Until now, the mortgage market has operated under free-market principles with a moderate level of government regulation, but this program would be a step toward government micromanagement. As a significant number of the loans now facing problems were made by irresponsible mortgage brokers using inaccurate and even false data, it would also signal that there are no real consequences for poor lending or borrowing practices.

Many of these refinanced mortgages will still be likely to default. The Congressional Budget Office (CBO) estimates that fully one-third of refinanced mortgages under H.R. 5830 will subsequently default. Historically, the risk of default is best measured by the size of a down payment. The smaller it is, the more likely that the borrower will walk away from the loan. While H.R. 5830 essentially gives owners of refinanced homes an amount equal to 10 percent of the current value of the house, this is a gift from the taxpayers, and the homeowner has none of his or her own savings at risk. Experience with similar "gift equity" programs already causing problems for the FHA shows that these loans have a default rate that is two to three times that of loans where the borrower has made a cash down payment.

The plan would reward two different groups of homeowners: those who took out a speculative loan they never had a chance of repaying in hopes of flipping the house in a rising market and those who fell into trouble through no fault of their own. Unfortunately, it is not always possible to distinguish borrowers by their intentions. But in providing relief, especially relief to homeowners/speculators, this bill sends a message that it is acceptable to renege on an obligation because a government buyout will cut your losses. The CBO estimates that, on average, each of the borrowers will receive a subsidy from the government equal to about $3,400.

H.R. 5830 merely duplicates the existing private program at a cost of billions of dollars and transfers all risk of default to the taxpayers.

Legislation Would Be Slow and Costly

Even if legislation were passed tomorrow, it is not possible to implement this plan rapidly. The FHA says that it does not currently have the people necessary to implement such a plan. It will take subsequent legislation to appropriate the funds needed to hire the appropriate additional federal work force, time to hire them, and more time yet to train them. In addition, mortgages must be refinanced individually. It will take a great deal of time to refinance the 1 million–2 million loans that supporters say could benefit. While supporters talk of refinancing loans in bulk, this is not possible under current laws or industry practice.

Closing costs for such refinancing can be expensive and are regulated by state laws. Distressed borrowers may not have the money available to pay them, and if the FHA covers the cost either directly or indirectly, either costs will climb or the number of potential beneficiaries will be reduced. Moreover, doing so would also be unfair to the responsible borrowers who refinance their homes.

The estimate for the number of homeowners who would be helped by H.R. 5830 continues to drop. First, supporters claimed that about 2 million homeowners would have loans refinanced. Since then, that number has steadily dropped, and now the CBO says that only 500,000 loans worth about $85 billion would be refinanced [by 2012].

Borrowers with legitimate problems are already being assisted by the voluntary Hope Now program, which is in place and operating. In the first quarter of 2008 alone, the Hope Now program assisted over 500,000 homeowners—the same number that the CBO says H.R. 5830 will assist over the next four years. The program is certain to help even more homeowners than H.R. 5830 in coming quarters because, unlike H.R. 5830, it is up and running. H.R. 5830 merely duplicates the existing private program at a cost of billions of dollars and transfers all risk of default to the taxpayers.

H.R 5830 will not stop foreclosures, even for many who would otherwise qualify. During the time it will take to put the program in place, mortgage servicers will be legally bound to follow the terms of the existing contract in case the refinancing falls through, including taking steps toward foreclosure. Further, as the CBO points out, many lenders will refuse to take part because it would require them to take heavy losses in order to participate. Other lenders who hold second mortgages on the same property could also block refinancings.

The continued pressure on Congress to "do something" about the large number of mortgages that are either in default or at risk of defaulting once their interest rates rise to market levels is extremely intense. Unfortunately, the Frank–Dodd H.R. 5830 really won't do anything to solve the problem.

What has worked to date is Hope Now, a voluntary, private-sector plan that allows homeowners who have the ability to pay a lower-cost loan to refinance their mortgages. Hope Now has assisted almost 1.4 million homeowners without major government intervention. Rather than pressing for massive new programs, legislators should allow one with proven results to do its work.

15

Lenders Should Not Be Allowed to Charge More for Mortgages in Poor Areas

Mary Kane

Mary Kane is a freelance business writer. Her work has appeared in Salon, Washington Post, Politico, Crain's Chicago Business, Newark Star-Ledger, *and other publications.*

Redlining is the practice of refusing to extend credit in poor and minority communities. Recently, in the aftermath of the mortgage market meltdown, some mortgage industry executives have embraced a policy that resembles redlining, by requiring higher fees for loans to borrowers purchasing homes in areas with a large number of foreclosures. Rather than following a policy that discriminates against minorities and those who live in poor areas, the loan industry needs to provide access to sustainable credit for all borrowers. As an alternative to charging poor people and minorities more money for their loans, the mortgage industry can require higher down payments in risky markets, and seek to assure that properties are appraised accurately.

In the middle of the housing boom, when virtually anyone could get credit, redlining wasn't even in the picture. It was an almost forgotten remnant of the past—a piece of lending history that involved lengthy legal battles and community organizing work to change a dark banking industry practice of denying credit based on where people lived or because of their race. But now, in the aftermath of the mortgage market melt-down, the cost and availability of credit for some borrowers is again becoming a concern—raising questions about whether a new kind of redlining is on the horizon.

A recent policy by the mortgage industry to charge higher fees for loans to borrowers in certain zip codes has been be-hind some of the concerns. It quickly led to charges of redlin-ing and violations of fair housing laws. That reignited old battles over access to credit—fights that housing advocates thought they had settled years earlier.

If the notion of extending or pricing credit based on a borrower's neighborhood sounds suspiciously like the redlining practices of old ... that's because it is another form of redlining, plain and simple.

Fighting Battles of the Past

Those advocates—the veterans of many past housing wars—responded swiftly, and aggressively, though no one predicted during the housing boom that the lending industry might even consider going down this road again. They formed alli-ances with realtor groups, and they challenged moves by lend-ers to make credit more costly or unavailable to certain groups of borrowers.

Their work paid off. Mortgage giant Fannie Mae [Federal National Mortgage Association] [recently] announced it would no longer assess loan risks by using a "declining markets des-ignation," meaning borrowers in certain geographic areas would pay more for loans because their communities show a higher rate of foreclosures, short sales and falling home val-ues. Fannie Mae, Freddie Mac [Federal Home Loan Mortgage Corporation], other lenders and private insurers have been us-ing the designation, as part of their automated underwriting systems. In some cases, a borrower doesn't know whether he resides in such a market until he applies for the loan.

If the notion of extending or pricing credit based on a borrower's neighborhood sounds suspiciously like the redlining practices of old, in which lenders refused to lend money in poor and minority communities, well, that's because it is another form of redlining, plain and simple, fair housing advocates say. Even though Fannie Mae has agreed to no longer use different underwriting standards for borrowers in high foreclosure areas, other lenders and insurers still employ the practice.

"It's our position that loan underwriting based on zip codes is a modern form of redlining," said David Berenbaum, executive vice president of the National Community Reinvestment Coalition, which represents fair housing groups. "I don't have a problem with lenders looking closely at the economics of the marketplace to ensure they are able to do business and are able to lend. But they need to do it in a way that doesn't have a discriminatory impact on neighborhoods and on certain groups of borrowers. This is just sort of a knee-jerk reaction to a difficult marketplace."

Gregory Squires, a George Washington University sociology professor who has studied predatory lending and redlining practices warned, "This should have set off alarm bells."

Black and Latino borrowers were far more likely to take out high-priced subprime loans than white borrowers, even when their credit scores were similar, research shows.

The Mortgage Meltdown Plays Itself Out

The fight over the policy shows how contentious things may get over access to credit as the mortgage meltdown shakes out. In many ways, lending to low-income and minority borrowers has come full circle—from redlining practices that denied them access to loans in 1950s and 1960s, to the "democratization of credit" in the 1990s that led to a credit glut and predatory lending, or reverse redlining, as Squires has described it.

Mortgage brokers and lenders began aggressively marketing subprime loans in the same neighborhoods once written off by traditional lenders, selling high-rate mortgages with hidden costs and fees. In neighborhoods long cut off from credit, these transactions, involving readily available mortgage money, often took place door to door, or by word-of-mouth spread through local churches.

With so many loans gone bad, the subprime market no longer exists.

Black and Latino borrowers were far more likely to take out high-priced subprime loans than white borrowers, even when their credit scores were similar, research shows.

This kind of lending came well before the housing bubble that began in 2005. That was when the subprime practices and lax underwriting spread to the rest of the mortgage market—especially in California, Florida, Nevada and other areas with hot housing markets that attracted investors, house-flippers and mostly prime borrowers.

With so many loans gone bad, the subprime market no longer exists. Wall Street investors, accused of turning a blind eye to subprime abuses in their pursuit of profits, are wary of providing capital for new loans. As lending standards tighten, first-time home buyers and borrowers with modest incomes now sometimes find themselves priced out of the mortgage market, even with the falling values that make some homes more affordable.

Credit Will Be Hard to Get

Once the credit squeeze eases, however, it's still not clear that the problems with loan pricing will end. The declining markets designation is just one example of how the market may have changed for good as a result of the housing collapse.

Housing advocates fear that all the progress made in four decades of fair housing fights will be set back significantly. The zip code controversy, they say, shows that borrowers with modest incomes could wind up paying higher prices or find mortgages or refinancing out of reach, directly as a result of speculation and lax lending standards among lenders and prime borrowers at the top of the market.

Every single pillar of the market has to be rethought. We're back to the drawing board and we're not sure how all this is going to play out.

"It's all quite disturbing," said Patricia McCoy, a University of Connecticut law professor who has studied subprime securitization. "We're on this precipice of another transformation in the mortgage market. Every single pillar of the market has to be rethought. We're back to the drawing board and we're not sure how all this is going to play out. It's a fairly precarious time for fair lending."

Adding to the uncertainty is the fact that even as the future of lending opens up to debate, its past is being reconsidered.

Some Blame Government Regulations

Some lenders and investors contend that the subprime mess stemmed from the financial industry being forced by government regulations, like the Community Reinvestment Act [CRA], to make bad loans in poor neighborhoods. At mortgage banking conferences, academic seminars and in the blogosphere, the notion has taken hold and grown in the same way as an urban myth does.

The CRA was created by Congress in 1977, as a way to combat redlining. It required banks to make sure credit was available in the communities in which they operated. In the 1990s, CRA ratings for banks took on increasing importance, with regulators citing them when institutions applied for mergers or expansions. Regulators could deny a bank acquisition of another financial institution based on a poor CRA rating.

According to the CRA theory, advocacy groups like ACORN [Association of Community Organizations for Reform Now] complained about redlining and pushed regulators into pressuring banks and lenders to make the bad loans.

Stan Liebowitz, an economics professor at the University of Texas-Dallas, called CRA regulations "the real scandal" of subprime lending in a recent *New York Post* column: From the current hand-wringing, you'd think that the banks came up with the idea of looser underwriting standards on their own, with regulators just asleep on the job. In fact, it was the regulators who relaxed these standards—at the behest of community groups and "progressive" political forces.

Blame the Political Left

In the *New York Sun*, economist Jerry Bowyer contended that "the fault lies with the small army of hard-left political hustlers who spent the early 1990s pushing risky mortgages on home lenders."

Housing advocates find the argument absurd. Some believe lenders are just using the CRA criticism to fend off future lending requirements and to avert blame for the subprime mess.

"This is the big lie," Berenbaum said. "There's been absolutely no pressure from advocacy organizations to expand home ownership by underwriting risky loans. That is just so far from the truth."

Contentious arguments over fair lending have a long history, going back to when the federal Fair Housing Act was passed outlawing discrimination in housing, one week after the assassination of Martin Luther King Jr. in 1968. But the law didn't end battles over the denial of credit.

In the late 1980s, the *Atlanta Journal and Constitution* published "The Color of Money," documenting racial discrimination in mortgage lending. In 1994, Chevy Chase Federal Savings Bank reached a settlement with the Justice Department over allegations that it failed to make loans in black neighborhoods in Washington and suburban Prince Georges County, Md.

As subprime loan brokers began flooding poor neighborhoods in the 1990s, consumer advocates and legal-aid lawyers complained, but the lending continued. In the mid-1990s, Associates First Capital Corp. earned $19,000 in fees by flipping an initial $20 loan 10 times over four years, to an illiterate borrower who signed his loan papers with an X. Citigroup purchased the Associates in 2000 and continued to make subprime loans.

Recently, fair housing groups have brought suits over lenders refusing to make loans for less than $100,000, or for denying "rowhouse loans" in Baltimore.

Credit shouldn't always be available for everyone. For some people, it won't be the right time in their lives to take on a mortgage.

Lenders Should Strive for Sustainable Credit

As the market restructures, industry leaders Fannie Mae and Freddie Mac will be under great financial pressure to provide mortgage money and still cover their costs, McCoy said. Asking for higher down payments in declining markets and careful use of accurate appraisals can address those concerns adequately, she believes. No one wants lenders to go back to making risky loans, but they also don't have to add on fees out of fear. "I'm not crazy about targeting zip codes and jacking up interest rates," she said.

Lenders and housing advocates should work toward access to sustainable credit—loans that a borrower can handle. It means that credit shouldn't always be available for everyone. For some people, it won't be the right time in their lives to take on a mortgage, which is a contrast to the relentless push for increased home ownership rates since the early 1990s, McCoy noted.

To Squires, changes in the market may also open the door to thinking about ways to support rental housing or alternative forms of housing like cooperatives.

The one thing certain about where the mortgage market is heading is that fights over lending tactics will continue. "These are constantly contentious political issues," Squires said. "As Saul Alinsky used to say, there are no permanent victories."

Housing advocates, however, are in a different position than they were at the beginning of the credit fights in the late 1960s, Berenbaum said. They are far more organized, sophisticated and able to respond quickly. They now work hand in hand with some in the lending industry.

They don't have much choice. As the mortgage industry enters its next phase, so will the battles over who gets access to credit and mortgage loans—and how much it will cost them. To the players in this fight, zip code designations are a reminder of the past, and a sign of what is soon to come.

Organizations to Contact

The editors have compiled the following list of organizations concerned with the issues debated in this book. The descriptions are derived from materials provided by the organizations. All have publications or information available for interested readers. The list was compiled on the date of publication of the present volume; the information provided here may change. Be aware that many organizations take several weeks or longer to respond to inquiries, so allow as much time as possible.

Fannie Mae
3900 Wisconsin Avenue, NW, Washington, DC 20016-2892
(202) 752-7000
Web site: www.fanniemae.com/index.jhtml

Fannie Mae was established by the U.S. government in 1938 to facilitate the flow of mortgage funds to communities throughout the country. A shareholder-owned company with a federal charter, Fannie Mae operates in America's secondary mortgage market to ensure that mortgage bankers and other lenders have access to funds to lend to home buyers.

Freddie Mac
8200 Jones Branch Drive, McLean, VA 22102
(703) 903-2000
Web site: www.freddiemac.com/index.html

Like Fannie Mae, Freddie Mac is a stockholder-owned company chartered by the federal government to help provide liquidity, stability, and affordability to the U.S. housing market. It does this by connecting the residential mortgage market to Wall Street and the investment community through its mortgage purchase, credit guarantee, and investment activities. The Freddie Mac Web site includes many resources and provides links to services of interest to home buyers.

Joint Center for Housing Studies at Harvard University
1033 Massachusetts Avenue, Cambridge, MA   02138
(617) 495-7908
Web site: www.jchs.harvard.edu

The Joint Center for Housing Studies analyzes relationships between housing markets and economic, demographic, and social trends, to provide leaders in government, business, and the nonprofit sector with the knowledge needed to develop effective housing policies and strategies. A list of recent publications located on the Joint Center's Web site includes the report *The State of the Nation's Housing 2008*, as well as information on affordable housing, rental housing, and the housing finance industry.

Mortgage Bankers Association
1331 L Street, NW, Washington, DC   20005
(202) 557-2700
Web site: www.mbaa.org

The Mortgage Bankers Association (MBA) is the national association representing the real estate finance industry. Its members include more than 2,400 companies involved in all aspects of real estate finance. The MBA publishes the monthly magazine *Mortgage Banking*.

National Association of Home Builders
1201 15th Street, NW, Washington, DC   20005
(800) 368-5242 • fax: (202) 266-8400
Web site: www.nahb.org

NAHB is a trade association promoting policies that make housing a national priority. The NAHB Web site includes resources on national housing issues, economic data, and political initiatives that impact the market for new houses.

National Coalition for the Homeless
2201 P Street, NW, Washington, DC   20037
(202) 462-4822

e-mail: info@nationalhomeless.org
Web site: www.nationalhomeless.org

The National Coalition for the Homeless is a national network of people who are committed to creating the systemic and attitudinal changes necessary to prevent and end homelessness. The Web site includes fact sheets on homelessness, its extent, causes, and people affected. It also includes publications on topics like rural homelessness, homeless children and youth in the education system, and domestic violence and homelessness.

National Fair Housing Alliance
1101 Vermont Avenue, NW, Washington, DC   20005
(202) 898-1661
Web site: www.nationalfairhousing.org

The National Fair Housing Alliance is a consortium of private, nonprofit fair housing organizations and state and local civil rights agencies with a common interest in combating housing discrimination. It works to ensure equal housing opportunity through leadership, education, advocacy and enforcement. The National Fair Housing Alliance Web site includes a resource page with a wide range of information relating to housing, discrimination and the law. Full text of federal documents such as the Truth in Lending Act and the Community Reinvestment Act can be downloaded.

**National Housing Conference and the Center
for Housing Policy**
1801 K Street, NW, Washington, DC   20006-1301
(202) 466-2121 • fax: (202) 466-2122
Web site: www.nhc.org

The National Housing Conference is a nonprofit organization that promotes policies, programs, and legislation to provide affordable and suitable housing. It researches affordable housing challenges of working class families, and works to create awareness of the need for decent, affordable housing.

National Housing Institute
111 Dunnell Road, Suite 102, Maplewood, NJ 07040
(973) 763-0333
Web site: www.nhi.org

The National Housing Institute is a nonprofit organization concerned with social and economic equality, health, the environment, education, and sustainability. The institute promotes policies for decent, affordable housing and strong communities.

U.S. Department of Housing and Urban Development (HUD)
451 7th Street, SW, Washington, DC 20410
(202) 708-1112
Web site: www.hud.gov

HUD is the U.S. government agency charged with increasing home ownership, supporting community development, and increasing access to affordable housing.

Bibliography

Books

Sumit Agarwal

Household Credit Usage: Personal Debt and Mortgages. New York: Palgrave Macmillan, 2007.

Atlantic Publishing Company

The Complete Dictionary of Mortgage & Lending Terms Explained Simply: What Smart Investors Need to Know. Ocala, FL: Author, 2008.

Richard Bitner

Confessions of a Subprime Lender: An Insider's Tale of Greed, Fraud, and Ignorance. Hoboken, NJ: Wiley, 2008.

Rachel G. Bratt, Michael E. Stone, and Chester W. Hartman

A Right to Housing: Foundation for a New Social Agenda. Philadelphia: Temple University Press, 2006.

Anthony M. Carr

Real Estate Investing Made Simple: A Commonsense Approach to Building Wealth. New York: American Management Association, 2005.

Chip Cummings

The Mortgage Myths: 77 Secrets That Will Save You Thousands on Home Financing. Hoboken, NJ: Wiley, 2008.

Blanche Evans

Bubbles, Booms, and Busts: Make Money in Any Real Estate Market. New York: McGraw-Hill, 2007.

June Fletcher	*House Poor: How to Buy and Sell Your Home Come Bubble or Bust.* New York: Collins, 2006.
June Fletcher	*House Poor: Pumped Up Prices, Rising Rates, and Mortgages on Steroids: How to Survive the Coming Housing Crisis.* New York: Collins, 2005.
Edward M. Gramlich	*Subprime Mortgages: America's Latest Boom and Bust.* Washington, DC: Urban Institute Press, 2007.
Peter Hartcher	*Bubble Man: Alan Greenspan and the Missing 7 Trillion Dollars.* New York: Norton, 2006.
Marc Labonte	*U.S. Housing Prices: Is There a Bubble?* Washington, DC: Congressional Information Service, Library of Congress, 2005.
Alice LaPlante	*Buying a Home.* Palo Alto, CA: Planning Shop, 2007.
Charles R. Morris	*The Trillion Dollar Meltdown: Easy Money, High Rollers, and the Great Credit Crash.* New York: PublicAffairs, 2008.
Charles R. Morris	*Money, Greed, and Risk: Why Financial Crises and Crashes Happen.* New York: Times Business, 1999.
John A. Rubino	*How to Profit from the Coming Real Estate Bust: Money-Making Strategies for the End of the Housing Bubble.* Emmaus, PA: Rodale, 2003.

Robert J. Shiller   *The Subprime Solution: How Today's Global Financial Crisis Happened and What to Do About It*. Princeton, NJ: Princeton University Press, 2008.

Joseph E. Stiglitz, Aaron S. Edlin, and J. Bradford DeLong   *The Economists' Voice: Top Economists Take on Today's Problems*. New York: Columbia University Press, 2008.

Guy Stuart   *Discriminating Risk: The U.S. Mortgage Lending Industry in the Twentieth Century*. Ithaca, NY: Cornell University Press, 2003.

John R. Talbott   *Sell Now!: The End of the Housing Bubble*. New York: St. Martin's Griffin, 2006.

Mark Zandi   *Financial Shock: A 360 Degree Look at the Subprime Mortgage Implosion and How to Avoid the Next Financial Crisis*. Harlow: Financial Times Press, 2008.

Articles

Joe Adler   "Housing Gets Crowded Off Candidates' Front Burners," *American Banker*, May 9, 2005.

Matthew Bandyk   "A Storm of Foreclosures; The Number of Homes Facing Foreclosure More Than Doubled in a Year," *U.S. News & World Report*, April 29, 2008.

Matthew Bandyk   "Poll: Americans Frozen by Housing Crisis," *U.S. News & World Report*, April 14, 2008.

Business Wire   "A Year into the Mortgage Meltdown, New Report Analyzes Housing Market Crisis and Federal Response," June 25, 2008.

Alice Z. Cuneo   "What Housing Crisis? Realtors' Ads Defy Reality; Despite a Nationwide Meltdown, Industry Says Now Is the Time to Buy," *Advertising Age*, January 28, 2008.

Mark Davis   "Animal Shelters Overcrowded Due to Housing Crisis," *Atlanta Journal-Constitution*, June 27, 2008.

Amilda Dymi   "Study: Foreclosure and Debt Haunting American Consumers," *National Mortgage News*, January 21, 2008.

Mark Farmer   "Build to Last: The Future of the Residential Development Sector Depends on Its Ability to Withstand Choked Lending, Reduced Sales and Debt Legacy," *Property Week*, May 30, 2008.

Mark Friedman   "Standards Tighten Among Lenders: Tougher Rules Contribute to Slowing Home Sales in Arkansas," *Arkansas Business*, May 19, 2008.

Grand Rapids Press   "Indictments Snare 400 Real Estate Insiders; Justice Department Makes Mortgage Fraud Arrests, Lists Michigan as a 'Hotspot,'" June 20, 2008.

Michael Hudson   "The New Road to Serfdom," *Harper's*, May 2006.

Julie Kay   "Empty Homes Spur Cities' Suits," *Fulton County Daily Report*, May 13, 2008.

G. Jeffrey MacDonald   "These Banks Step in to Avert Foreclosure," *Christian Science Monitor*, June 30, 2008.

Maclean's   "Florida Invasion," May 26–June 2, 2008.

Eileen Markey   "Mortgage Crisis Weighs Heavily on Poor: Buried in Nation's Financial Woes Is a Serious Moral Issue, Catholic Leaders Say," *National Catholic Reporter*, April 18, 2008.

Eileen Markey   "Subprime Loan Crisis Swamps Agencies: Housing Advocates Scramble to Assist Clients Facing Foreclosure," *National Catholic Reporter*, February 22, 2008.

Allan I. Mendelowitz and John D. Koch   "Viewpoint: Fixing Supply and Demand." *American Banker*, April 18, 2008.

Janet Morrissey   "Still Searching for a Bottom in the Housing Crisis; Bears Warn the Rebound Could Be Eight Years Away." *Investment News*, June 9, 2008.

Janet Morrissey   "Housing Bailout Faces Tough Road; Proposal Would Offer Up to $300B in Loan Guarantees to Stem 500,000 Foreclosures," *Investment News*, May 12, 2008.

Luke Mullins   "How Youngstown is Tackling the Housing Crisis," *U.S. News & World Report*, April 29, 2008.

National Mortgage News   "Top Subprime Lenders in 2007," May 12, 2008.

Terence M. O'Sullivan   "Pull Plug on Homebuilder Bailouts: Foreclosure Prevention Act of 2008 Would Reward Businesses for Bad Behavior at Taxpayers' Expense." *Los Angeles Business Journal*, April 28, 2008.

Kimberly Palmer   "Not Making It Like Mom and Dad," *U.S. News & World Report*, July 7, 2008.

Peter Schroeder   "Survey: 26% of Cities Hit with Bigger Debt Costs Due to Subprime Crisis," *The Bond Buyer*, March 12, 2008.

Paul Shigley   "Fixing Foreclosure: Local Governments Try to Cope with the Housing Crisis." *Planning*, June, 2008.

Robert J. Shiller   "Bubble, Bubble, Where's the Housing Bubble?" Brookings Papers on Economic Activity No. 1, 2006.

Lew Sichelman   "Consultant: Housing Crisis Issues Go Beyond 'Sticks and Bricks': Viewing Housing as 'A Community Issue' That Goes Beyond Builders, the Lenders Who Finance Them and Their Buyers," *National Mortgage News*, July 23, 2007.

Aissatou Sidime   "Refinancing Predatory Mortgage Loans: New Fund Rescues Homeowners from Usurious Interest Rates," *Black Enterprise*, September 2006.

Robert Ver Bruggen   "Straw Predators: For the Mortgage Meltdown, the Left Deserves a Share of Blame," *National Review*, May 5, 2008.

Andrew Ward   "Subprime Crisis Morphs into Budget Crisis as States Feel Pinch," *The Bond Buyer*, April 15, 2008.

Mortimer B. Zuckerman   "Did Someone Say Bubble?" *U.S. News & World Report*, May 8, 2006.

Index

A

Accoustic Home Loans, 35
ACORN (Association of Community Organizations for Reform Now), 43, 102
Acorn Financial Justice Center, 8
Adjustable-rate mortgages (ARMs)
  Alan Greenspan and, 51
  defined, 11
  as factor in foreclosures, 87–88
  predatory lending practices and, 7, 52
  resets of, 67, 68, 74, 91
  sub-prime borrowers and, 50, 52
Alinsky, Saul, 104
American Banker (trade newspaper), 35
Ameriquest, 29
The American Prospect (magazine), 82
Arizona, 66
ARMs. *See* Adjustable-rate mortgages (ARMs)
Asset prices, 79–80
Associates First Capital Corp., 103
Association of Community Organizations for Reform Now (ACORN), 43, 102
Atlanta Journal and Constitution (newspaper), 103
Atlas, John, 38, 82, 83
Austin, Algernon, 54

B

Bailouts, mortgages, 92–96
Baltimore (MD), 8
Bank of Japan, 78

Banking, 39–42
Bartiromo, Maria, 53
Bear Stearns, 9, 35, 36, 77, 79
Berenbaum, David, 99, 102, 104
Bernanke, Ben, 45, 52–53
Birmingham (AL), 7, 8
Birmingham News (newspaper)
Boeri, Tito, 44
Bond rating agencies, 9
The Boston Globe (newspaper), 42
Boston (MA), 34, 61
Bowyer, Jerry, 102
Buffalo (NY), 82
Bush, George W., 38–39, 59, 64, 84
Bush administration, 42–43
Business Week (magazine), 8–9

C

Cabrini Green (public housing), 60
California, 8, 64, 82, 86–87, 100
Case-Shiller Home Price Index, 76
CBO (Congressional Budget Office), 93, 94, 95
CDOs (collateralized debt obligations), 9, 15–18
Center for Responsible Lending, 43
Chevy Chase Federal Savings Bank, 103
Chicago (IL), 60
Chrysler Corporation, 86
Citigroup, 103
Cleveland (OH), 8, 82
Clinton administration, 60, 69

CNBC (television channel), 53

Collateralized debt obligations (CDOs), 9, 15–18

Colorado, 86

Community Reinvestment Act (CRA), 40, 101–102

Commuters, 62, 63

Congressional Budget Office (CBO), 93, 94

Countrywide Financial Corporation, 8

CRA (Community Reinvestment Act), 40, 101–102

Credit, access to, 77, 98, 100–101, 104

D

DataVerify, 36

Debt obligations, collaterallized (CDOs), 9, 15–18

Deed of trust custom, 89–90

Defaults, 93-94, 96
  See also Foreclosures

Democratic Party, 43

"Democratization of credit," 99–100

Denver (CO), 88

Depository Institutions Deregulatory and Monetary Control Act, 40

Depressions. *See* Great Depression

Deregulation, banking industry, 39–42

Detroit (MI), 86, 88

District of Columbia, 69

Documentation, 11

Dodd, Christopher, 93, 96

Down payments, 93–94

Dreier, Peter, 38, 82, 83, 84

"Driving to qualify," 62

E

ECB (European Central Bank), 48

Egan, Conrad, 61

Elmer, Julie, 7

European Central Bank (ECB), 48

F

Fair, Ray, 53

Fair Housing Act, 102

Fairfax County (VA), 58, 61, 62, 63, 64

Fairfax housing authority, 61, 64

Fannie Mae (Federal National Mortgage Association)
  description, 14–15, 105
  Great Depression and, 39, 82–83
  loan policies of, 14, 15, 98, 99
  market restructuring and, 103
  purpose of, 14
  regulation of, 73–74
  Wall Street and, 36

Fannie Mae Foundation study, 69, 70

Fauquier County (VA), 62

FDIC (Federal Deposit Insurance Corporation), 39, 82

Fed (Federal Reserve System), 50, 51, 56, 76–80

Federal Bank of St. Louis, 50

Federal Deposit Insurance Corporation (FDIC), 39, 82

Federal Home Loan Bank System, 39, 82

Federal Home Loan Mortgage Corporation. *See* Freddie Mac (Federal Home Loan Mortgage Corporation)

Federal Housing Administration (FHA), 39, 40, 83, 92, 94

Federal National Mortgage Association. *See* Fannie Mae (Federal National Mortgage Association)

Federal Reserve System (Fed), 50, 51, 56, 76–80

FHA (Federal Housing Administration), 39, 40, 83, 92, 94

Financial Crimes Enforcement Network, 30

Financial literacy/illiteracy, 45, 46

"Financial services" industry, 83

First-Time Homebuyers Tax Credit (HBTC), 69, 70, 71, 75

Fixed-rate mortgages, 51–52, 91

Florida, 8, 34, 66, 82, 100

Ford Motor Company, 86

Foreclosures
    deed of trust states and, 89–90
    factors contributing to, 85–87
    falling property values and, 7, 82
    Frank-Dodd H.R. 5830 and, 95, 96
    in Memphis (TN), 88–90
    options to avoid, 87
    protection against, 8, 39, 69

4506T IRS form, 29, 30

Frank, Barney, 42, 92, 93, 96

Frank-Dodd H.R. 5830, 92–96

Fraud, mortgage, 30, 31, 36, 51

Freddie Mac (Federal Home Loan Mortgage Corporation)
    declining markets designation, use of, 98
    description, 14–15, 105
    fraud and, 52
    loan policies of, 14, 15, 98
    market restructuring and, 103
    regulation of, 73–74
    Wall Street and, 36

Frederick County (VA), 62

Free market ideology, conservative, 41

G

General Accounting Office, 56

General Motors, 86

Ginnie Mae (Government National Mortgage Association), 14

Goldman Sachs, 53

Government
    bailouts, 92–96
    banking regulation and, 39–41
    housing crisis and, 82–84
    regulation/deregulation, 39–41

Government National Mortgage Association. *See* Ginnie Mae (Government National Mortgage Association)

Graham Fisher & Company, 32

Gramlich, Edward M., 41–42

Great Depression, 39, 45, 48, 81–83

Greenlining Institute, 43

Greenspan, Alan
    fixed-rate mortgages and, 51–52
    interest rate policy of, 44, 45, 46–48
    sub-prime lending and, 42

Grunwald, Michael, 58

Guiso, Luigi, 44

H

Halper, Steve, 36

Harvard Joint Center for Housing Studies, 62

HBTC (First-Time Homebuyers Tax Credit), 69, 70, 71, 75

Hedge funds, 9

Heritage Foundation, 59

Hickory Hill (Memphis, TN neighborhood), 88–89

High-rise apartments, 60, 63, 64

Home Mortgage Disclosure Act, 40

Home prices, 13–14

Homebuyers Tax Credit, 69–70

Homeowners Loan Corporation, 39

Homeownership
  as the American dream, 39, 64–65, 75
  benefits of, 74–75
  George W. Bush and, 38–39

Hope Now Program, 95, 96

Hope VI public housing plan, 60

Housing
  affordability/prices, 58–65
  boom, 13
  bubble, 12, 100
  high density projects, 60, 63
  rent aid, 61–62
  slump, 66–67, 87
  voucher programs, 71–73
  workforce, 64

H.R. 5830, 92–96

HUD (U.S. Department of Housing and Urban Development), 72, 108

Hudgins, Cathy, 62

I

Illinois, 8, 86

"Inclusionary zoning," 64

Indiana, 82, 86

Inflation, 79

Inside Mortgage Finance (newsletter), 15

Interest rates, 45–47, 50, 51, 52, 89

Internal Revenue Service (IRS), 29, 30

IRS form 4506T, 29, 30

J

Japan, 78

Job losses, 86–87

John, David C., 92

Joint Center for Housing Studies at Harvard University, 106

K

Kané, Mary, 97

Keating, Charles, 40

"Keating Five," 40

Kerry, John F., 59

Keynes, John Maynard, 48

King, Austin, 8

King, Martin Luther, 102

L

Lawsuits, 8, 31–32

Lehman Bros., 35

Liebowitz, Stan, 102

Limits, credit, 11

Liquidity, 45, 46, 47, 78

Loans
  defaults on, 38, 67
  in jeopardy, 67–68??
  predatory, 7, 8, 89, 100
  printing money for, 76–80
  reset, 67, 68
  subprime, 10–19, 67
  See also Subprime mortgage crisis

Los Angeles (CA), 64

Low-Income Housing Tax Credit of 1986, 64

M

Makin, John H., 76
Markel, Sherri, 34
Maryland, 66
MBS. *See* Mortgage-backed securities (MBS)
McCain, John, 40, 55
McCoy, Patricia, 101, 104
Memphis (TN), 88–90
Merger mania, 40
Merrill Lynch, 35, 3736
Michigan, 86
Midwestern states, 86
Misrepresentation, 31
"Money Honey" (Maria Bartiromo), 53
Morgenson, Gretchen, 28
Mortgage-backed securities (MBS), 15–16, 83–84
Mortgage Bankers Association, 67, 86, 89, 106
Mortgage Lenders Network, 35
Mortgages
    bailouts for, 92–96
    fixed-rate, 51–52, 91
    Mortgage-backed securities (MBS), 15–16, 83–84
    mortgage fraud, 30, 31, 36, 51
    mortgage industry, 34, 35, 79, 83
    risks of, 12–13, 15, 47
    securitization of, 14–16, 45, 46, 83–84
    See also Adjustable-rate mortgages (ARMS); Subprime mortgage crisis
Muolo, Paul, 33

N

National Association of Home Builders, 106
National Coalition for the Homeless, 106–107
National Community Reinvestment Coalition, 43, 99
National Fair Housing Alliance, 107
National Housing Conference and the Center for Housing Policy, 107
National Housing Institute, 82, 108
National Mortgage News (weekly newspaper), 35
Neighborhood Housing Services, 43, 84
Nevada, 66, 100
New Century, 35
New York Post (newspaper), 102
New York Sun (newspaper), 102
New York Times (newspaper), 51
NIMBY ("not in my backyard"), 63
Nixon, Richard M., 60
Normura, 35
Norris, Floyd, 51

O

Obama, Barack, 54
Occidental College (Los Angeles, CA), 82
Ohio, 86
Ownit Mortgage, 35
Owns/Own-Nots, 59, 65

P

Path to Investing (educational Web site), 10
Paulson, Henry, 42
Peirce, Neil, 81
Penalties, prepayment, 11

"Penny for Housing" initiative, 64
Pittsburgh (PA), 82
Poole, William, 50, 51
Predatory loans, 7, 8, 89, 100
Prepayment penalties, 11
Prince Georges County (MD), 103
Printing money, 76–80
Private label issuance, 15
Progressive Policy Institute, 66, 69
Property values, 7
"Protecting Access to Safe Mortgage Act," 73
Proxmire, William, 40

R

Racial discrimination, 39–40, 54–56
Rates. *See* Adjustable-rate mortgages; Fixed-rate mortgages; Interest rates
Ratings, mortgages, 15–16
Real estate, 47–48, 65
RealtyTrac, 85
Recessions, 48, 78
Redlining, 39-40, 97-101
   See also Racial discrimination; Zip code designations
Refinancing, 89, 92–93, 94, 95
Reflation, 76–80
Regulation/deregulation, 39–41, 81–84
Regulations, zoning, 63
Rents, 72, 73
Reset, subprime loans, 67, 68, 74
Risks, mortgages, 12–13, 15, 47
Robert Taylor Homes (public housing), 60
Roosevelt, Franklin D., 58, 60
Rosner, Josh, 32

S

Savings-and-loan industry, 39, 40, 83
Schumer, Charles, 73
Schwendimann, Hans L., 85
Securitization, mortgages, 14–16, 31–32, 45, 83–84
Security, sense of, 75
Sigma events, 79
Smith, David, 61
S&P/Case-Shiller national home-price index, 13
Squires, Gregory, 99, 104
Stelzer, Irwin M., 49
Subprime mortgage crisis
   adjustable-rate mortgages and, 11, 12–13, 19
   causes of, 12–14, 28–32, 67–68
   collateralized debt obligation in, 15–18
   managing, 18–20
   securitization and, 14–16, 31–32, 45, 83–84
   subprime loans, definition of, 10–11
   Wall Street and, 35–37
   See also Mortgages; Wall Street
Subprime receivables (servicing rights), 37
Summers, Mike, 29, 30
Swicord, Jeff, 21

T

Tax credits, 64, 69–70
Tennessee, 66, 88–90
Thornberg, Christopher, 64
Treasury securities, 76–79
Truman, Harry, 33
Tustin (CA), 29

U

Unemployment, 86
U.S. Conference of Mayors, 82
U.S. Congress
    deregulation of banking, 40, 83
    housing assistance and, 60, 64–65
    redlining and, 101
    sub-prime lending and, 42, 68
U.S. Department of Housing and Urban Development (HUD), 72, 108
U.S. Treasury Department, 30
Utt, Ron, 59–60

V

Veritax Inc., 29, 30
Veterans Administration, 39
Vienna Metro station (Fairfax, VA), 63
Voucher programs, 71–73, 75

W

Walker, Dagney Johnson, 7
Wall Street
    deregulation of, 82–84
    lawsuits and, 32
    reflation and, 76
    subprime crisis, role in, 35–37, 100
Warrenton (VA), 62
Washington, D.C., 69, 70, 103
Weinstein, Paul Jr., 66
Wells Fargo Bank, 50
Winchester (VA), 62

Z

Zip code designations, 101, 103, 104, 98
    See also Racial discrimination; Redlining
Zoning regulations, 63, 64